You Got This! Critical Thinking in Action

Unlock Clear Thinking, Beat Bias, and Make Better Life Decisions — All in 31 Days or Less with a Proven Plan to Strengthen Logic and Solve Real Problems

Jay Sissom

For discounted bulk purchases of this book for your company, association, or conference, visit jaysissom.com.

To book Jay Sissom for interviews or speaking, visit jaysissom.com.

ISBN 979-8-9992227-1-8 (paperback)

ISBN 979-8-9992227-2-5 (hardback)

For Laura, who proved that sometimes the best decisions are the ones you don't have to think twice about—like marrying someone who laughs at your terrible jokes (sometimes) and puts up with all your hobbies. The decision to marry you was by far the smartest one I ever made.

For Allie, Brian, Jade and Clayton, I'm the luckiest stepdad to have you in my life.

For Blair, your G-Dawg has enjoyed watching you learn how to navigate this big world and looks forward to helping you as you grow into an adult. I'm doing what I can to make this world a better place for you and your generation.

Contents

Introduction

Welcome to Your Thinking Upgrade

Think for yourselves and let others enjoy the privilege to do so too.

Voltaire

F rom the moment you open your eyes to start a new day, right up until you turn out the lights to end that day, you're constantly making decisions. This myriad of daily decisions can involve deciding what to eat for breakfast, what to wear for work or school, how to prioritize your to-do list, when to take your lunch break, which route to take on your way home, or when to have a difficult conversation with a colleague. Making these decisions can be overwhelming, confusing, and stressful, and you might feel regretful if your decisions don't yield the desired outcome. However, before you're too hard on yourself for "not thinking clearly" and before you lean into the negatives of this so-called decision fatigue, take a beat to realize that most decisions you make, regardless of the outcome, involve putting the concept of critical thinking into action. If you've made a decision as simple as grabbing your umbrella before leaving your house to avoid getting caught in the rain after checking your weather apps and noticing a few dark clouds looming, you've used critical thinking to make everyday decisions. The next step on your path to upgrading your thinking requires you to activate and exercise your critical thinking abilities consciously.

Why Critical Thinking Matters Now More Than Ever

Critical thinking involves gathering information from a variety of sources and processing this information by logically analyzing, evaluating, and interpreting it to reach a conclusion or make a decision. Critical thinking might seem like an abstract concept that often gets thrown into the pop psychology ether without leaving anything to grip onto. However, the existence of one major factor in society today justifies us holding onto our critical thinking skills for dear life and honing them to the sharpest point, and that factor is the information overload.

The world is rapidly evolving in terms of technology and the ways in which information is created, shared, and consumed. We live in an attention economy where your consumption of, distribution of, and engagement with content is monetized to the point where you can easily get caught up in the 24-hour news cycle, scroll endlessly on social media, or mistake AI-generated content for original work. This endless stream of information can lead to "infobesity," where you start to feel overwhelmed and anxious about being constantly bombarded by details. The consequence of getting sucked into the vortex of the information overload is that it doesn't give your brain the opportunity to process and sort the information you take in to be able to make a logical decision on what is correct based on the evidence presented. This can cause you to go down the rabbit hole of giving into your biases and only paying attention to information that supports your opinion.

Losing the ability to discern between fact and fiction or critically evaluate evidence and its source might've led you to make a poor decision in the past, such as impulsively buying an item online because a message that there were only two of the items left popped up on your screen. You might've decided to quit your job for another one based on your gut feeling, only for it not to work out as planned. You might've reacted negatively to a post that cropped up on your social media feed because it didn't agree with your opinions. These everyday examples show that the stakes of not using critical thinking to guide your decisions have high stakes and real-life consequences for your finances, career, and relationships. Adapting your thinking style to turn uncertainty or a lack of knowledge in an area into a learning opportunity is how you leverage your critical thinking skills to stay mentally afloat amidst the current information overload in society, and whenever you feel overwhelmed by a decision you have to make in your personal life.

The 31-Day Challenge: How This Book Works

Critical thinking is a skill that can be practiced and improved upon, it's not a gift or talent that some are not graced with. At this moment, you possess the inherent ability to perfect your critical thinking skills, and doing so will only enhance your intellectual abilities. Critical thinking is the key that unlocks the door to becoming a better problem solver, an analytical thinker, being more open-minded and creative, making logical decisions, and communicating more effectively. Once you tap into your critical thinking abilities and build upon this skill, it will change the way you make decisions, solve problems, and your perspective on the world.

You might be asking what exactly a "thinking upgrade" involves. Consider that a fitness or health upgrade requires you to implement small and consistent changes or habits into your daily life to streamline your diet, exercise, and healthcare routine. Similarly, incorporating certain processes and habits into your thinking processes can streamline how you make decisions every day and make your life more efficient. The structure of this book allows you to use the 31 exercises described throughout to set aside 31 days to consciously and methodically build your critical thinking muscle. The cumulative effect of applying the one powerful idea or skill included in each practical exercise or challenge will leave you with critical thinking tools and habits and a clarity of thought that you never had before going on this journey.

Each exercise is designed to challenge you intellectually but work through them at your own pace because life happens, and you're here to enhance the adaptability and flexibility of your thinking habits. You'll start with a mental clean-up to declutter your mind of the distractions of the information overload and learn how to prioritize and categorize your thoughts and knowledge. Next, you'll uncover how your unconscious thoughts and mental habits impact the way you think, and how to overcome these obstacles to critical thinking. Mastering how to ask the right questions about a problem is the next step to becoming an effective critical thinker, and this sense of curiosity will be elaborated upon in relation to the evaluation of evidence. The concepts of logic and systems thinking, and decision-making tools will be explored as you strengthen your critical thinking capabilities. Using the power of critical thinking to collaborate with others and think clearly when you're under pressure are skills you'll learn over the next 31 days.

By the end of this voyage of self-improvement, you'll be equipped with tools that are all action and no fluff. You'll be able to apply these critical thinking tips in your actual life, whether it be making high-stakes decisions in the boardroom, having a casual conversation about current events with a friend, or deciding to put down that deposit on your dream home.

Exercise 1: Measuring Your Current Thinking Style

Before you go about upgrading your thinking, let's start by identifying your thinking style with the first of the 31 challenges to help you reach your potential as a critical thinker. Self-awareness and habit recognition are important components of critical thinking. Answer the questions below by thinking about how you prefer to tackle a problem and read about the corresponding thinking style to determine your current thinking style. There is no right or wrong answer, so view this exercise as an opportunity to learn more about yourself instead of judging your choices.

1. Do you see a problem as a puzzle to solve? Do you tend to see the hidden ideas or concepts that make up the bigger picture of the problem? If so, you might be an "abstract" thinker.

2. Are you systematic and methodical when solving a problem? Do you create steps to follow and evaluate the quality of your method at each step? If so, you may just be an "analytical" thinker.

3. Do you prefer to only deal with the undisputed facts and evidence to solve a problem? Do you tend to take a linear or literal approach when solving problems? If so, you probably fit into the "concrete" thinking category.

4. Do you tend to search for alternative or "out of the box" solutions to a problem? Do you prefer to mull over a problem to consider it more deeply before coming up with a solution? If so, you're likely a "creative" thinker.

5. Do you prefer to narrow down the problem to its bare bones and come up with one solid solution? Are you a better problem solver when there are many pieces of evidence or information involved? If so, you might be a "convergent" thinker.

6. Do you favor having multiple viable solutions to a problem to choose from? Do you solve problems using mind maps or spider web diagrams, where the problem is the central focus and the solutions branch out of it? If so, then you're a "divergent" thinker.

Now that you've identified what kind of thinker you might be, start a journal to begin growing as a critical thinker. Use this journal to note down your current thinking habits, what you learn along the way that you wish you could change about your current thinking style, and the wins you accumulate as you conquer the challenges on your critical thinking journey.

Chapter One

Clear the Clutter

Building a Thinking Foundation

The trouble with having an open mind, of course, is that people will insist on coming along and trying to put things in it.

Terry Pratchett

Learning how to apply critical thinking to scenarios or decisions in your life can be likened to building a house, a comfortable place you can go to gather your thoughts, weigh the evidence, analyze it, and make a decision about the validity of that information. A house is made up of many components, for example, the foundation, the materials used, the walls, the rooms, the decor, and the touches that make the home uniquely yours. Building this "house" to enable you to think critically requires a strong foundation. In this chapter, we'll explore how to declutter the acres of land that will be used to lay the foundation to house the skills you build to think more critically. We'll delve into why a cluttered mind can lead to a lack of clarity in your thinking, how to overcome this clutter, how to find logic at the end of the tunnel of mental clutter, and how to develop habits to help you distill your thoughts and use critical thinking effectively every day.

Mental Clean-Up—Spotting the Noise in Your Thoughts

Mental clutter is a common feeling that can hinder your clear thinking daily. For example, you might feel like there's a constant voice in your head reminding you of the multiple tasks you need to get done for your family and yourself as soon as you wake up. You might feel overwhelmed and hopeless by reading your news feed before you leave for work in the morning. Your behavior during an awkward date or work meeting from the previous week might be playing on a loop in your mind. These thoughts seem to be endless and increasingly urgent to the point where it feels like your mind is shouting at you like a broker in the middle of Wall Street. If you've experienced this feeling of being mentally clouded and swamped by the deluge of noise in your mind telling you what you need to do, read, be, buy, or stop, then you're not alone.

Noisy thoughts are something everyone deals with to some degree. You might feel like the clutter will never be cleared from your mind or that it's impossible to be there for everyone and get everything on your eternal to-do list done in time. Mental clutter usually originates from overthinking about your past actions or omissions, feeling fear when thinking about the tasks or obligations that lie ahead of you, negative as-sumptions about yourself or your abilities, and the general information overload that exists on our electronic devices due to the general hyper connectivity of today's world.

Negative thought cycles that can cause mental clutter include reflecting negatively on your past decisions and actions, feeling anxious about the future, seeing yourself and your life in a negative light, and creating to-do lists that are impractical and impossible to execute. The risks of letting the noise consume you mentally are serious and include the emergence of feelings of anxiety and low self-esteem. Your physical health can also be impacted because you might feel you're always in a rush to get things done so you neglect healthy eating, self-care, and good sleep hygiene. Avoiding the pitfalls of mental clutter and its impact on your mental clarity requires the same mindset as clearing the brush and rubble from that piece of land you plan to build your critical thinking foundation house on: you have to start somewhere.

Eliminating that constant feeling of restlessness, a lack of focus, and like your mind is overloaded with information and tasks to complete requires a plan of action that suits your lifestyle and personality. Clearer thinking and, eventually, critical thinking, are just on the other side of the mountain of mental clutter that you can easily conquer with techniques to quieten down your mental chaos. The first such technique is using a journal to become more mindful about slipping out of the thought tornado seemingly whirling around in your mind. Consciously choosing the book, pen, and space you'll use to journal the thoughts in your head can help to mentally slow down and process your thoughts. The next method is to spend some meaningful time in solitude without people or devices in reach to give yourself a chance to gather your thoughts without interruptions or adding to the pile of mental clutter. If being alone isn't working, it might help to do the opposite and talk to a trusted friend, family member, or professional to verbalize what factors you think are causing your mental clutter. Changing your diet and increasing your daily movement through exercise can enhance your mental clarity.

Clearing out junk food, keeping to an exercise routine, and eating at regular times can help you feel calmer and more in control of your thoughts. Taking time to discover a new hobby and cutting down on the amount of time you spend on social media or swirling in the 24-hour news cycle can help to remove brain fog and distractions from productive and peaceful thoughts. When trying out the above techniques to declutter your mind, focus on moving forward instead of pausing your progress by focusing on past decisions and actions that you might regret or be ashamed of.

Exercise 2: 5-Minute Mind Sweep

This exercise will help you declutter your mind to take the next steps to laying a strong foundation for becoming a critical thinker. The 5-minute Mind Sweep can be used as a precursor to or in conjunction with any of the techniques described above. The objective is to identify the thoughts clouding your mind, their validity and importance, and how to deal with them. Approach the task with the desire for awareness of your thoughts and how to filter them.

1. This exercise is supposed to take five minutes and should help you avoid overthinking. Start your mind sweep by sitting with your journal in a peaceful space in your home or office.

2. Write down the thoughts that pop into your mind. Don't worry about organizing them just yet, just let everything flow and pour out as if you've turned on a mental faucet to empty the clutter. Now that you've written everything down, there should be less mental pressure on you to remember every small detail because you've written it down. You're already taking control of your mental clarity.

3. Categorize your thoughts by eliminating irrelevant or negative thoughts. Ask yourself questions like "Is this still relevant?", "Was this thought process in my control?", "Was this thought based on an emotional response?", or "Was this serious enough for me to spend mental real estate on it?". Before discarding negative thoughts, consider the situation you were in when you had them and reflect on this during the exercise to avoid repeating the negative thought cycle.

4. Prioritize your thoughts into what is actionable in the near future (i.e., in the next five minutes or next month), which thoughts are purely emotional responses to situations, and thoughts that are irrelevant and clouding your mind. For example, thinking about wanting to eat healthier or having to prepare for a family reunion are actionable, whereas a thought that you could get fired for not working on the weekends because everyone else at the office does is an unnecessary thought.

5. Use your takeaway list as the actual to-do list of what thoughts to act on and what to discard. Do the five-Minute Mind Sweep once a week for a positive mindset.

The Basics of Logic—What It Is and Why It Works

Once you've cleared the debris or mental clutter from the piece of land you've chosen to build your critical thinking house upon, the next step is to learn about logic and how to apply it in your thinking. Logic involves the act of reasoning, which requires you to make claims or arguments and use evidence to draw inferences or conclusions based on the evidence. Logic is like the first layer of cement laid upon the foundation of your critical thinking house. Using logic to make decisions also requires you to learn to tell the difference between good reasoning and bad reasoning to make accurate and clear decisions. This stage is where aspects like logical fallacies and inherent biases can trick your brain into choosing the easiest path, to telling yourself what you want to hear instead of making the correct decision.

Logical arguments start with a premise, which then moves towards gathering evidence based on that premise and ends with you coming up with a conclusion that proves the premise true or false. The relationship between your premise and conclusion depends on how you choose to reason through the evidence you have. You can choose to use deductive reasoning (top-down reasoning), where you move from a general premise to come up with a specific conclusion. For example, your premise might be that all humans are mortal. The evidence for your premise is that you're a human mortal and your friends are also both human and mortal. Your conclusion is, therefore, that you're mortal because you're human. Inductive reasoning (cause-and-effect reasoning) is where you move from a specific premise to make a general conclusion based on the evidence. Continuing with our previous example, our specific premise is that you're human and mortal. The evidence you have is that humans are mortal. Your conclusion is therefore that all humans are mortal. With deductive reasoning, the conclusion is always true if the premise is true, i.e., the general proves the specific. With inductive reasoning, the conclusion might be true if the evidence or your observations align with the premise.

Both types of reasoning have their pros and cons and apply to different situations. For example, if you check the weather and use that to decide whether or not to wear a sweater, you've used inductive reasoning because you've concluded that it might be generally cold during the day based on the specific premise of needing a sweater in cold weather and the evidence of checking your weather app. If you've ever conducted market research at your job, you've used deductive reasoning because you've gathered evidence based on a questionnaire resulting from the premise that customers generally act in a certain way. You then used the evidence to draw a specific conclusion about your customers.

Using logic to weigh evidence before making decisions can become somewhat of a superpower as part of your critical thinking arsenal because it helps you cut through the emotional background noise that can cloud your judgment. Avoiding these mental traps and choosing logic and rationality can keep you level-headed, even when you're under pressure to make high stakes decisions. Logic and the negative consequences of not using it will be explored in more detail in Chapter 5 of this book.

Exercise 3: The Logic of Memes

Memes have become an important communication tool, especially in the current attention and technology driven economy. Memes capture pop culture moments, society's thoughts on them, and can add a sense of humor to otherwise serious situations, even if this humor is sometimes dark. They rely on a sense of common consciousness or logic about a topic to go "viral" and gain popularity. A popular meme that uses logic to denote humor is the Venn diagram meme (Figure 1), where two or three logically connected things that are unlikely to occur at the same time are joined together using a Venn diagram.

Exercise your logical reasoning skills by researching popular memes, headlines, or advertisements and examining the reasoning behind them that makes them funny or effective. Biased news headlines often abandon logic in favor of making one party look more legitimate than the other to garner an emotional reaction from the reader. Using logic to identify these instances is where your critical thinking skills will serve you well amidst the information overload and 24-hour news cycle.

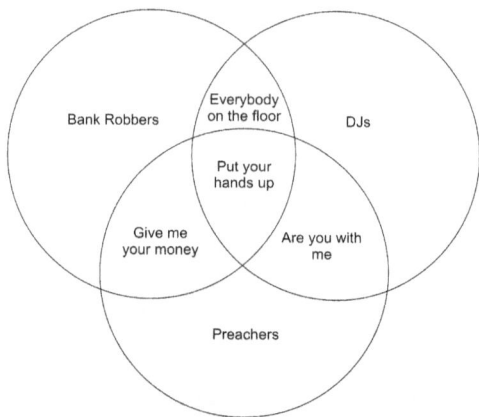

Figure 1: Meme

Daily Mindset Habits for Clearer Thinking

As part of the process of decluttering your mind and building a strong foundation of logical reasoning skills, developing healthy mindset habits can help you make the best of your brain's critical thinking abilities. Just like exercise and a balanced diet nourish your body, a healthy mindset can keep your mind clear, sharp, rational, and adaptable. Your physical and mental health work in tandem to help your brain, immune system, and nervous system function properly. You might notice that when you think negatively, you start to feel stressed, anxious. This can impact your physical well-being. Life is far from linear, and curve balls or difficult decisions await you at every turn, so it's essential to train yourself to choose a healthy and positive mindset to better cope with and navigate any bumps in the road.

Encouraging a healthy mindset in the context of critical thinking means being aware of yourself and the world around you. You want to stimulate your mind to go from accepting or consuming information to inquiring and analyzing instead. Achieving this mental sense of growth means testing out and eventually adopting a few healthy mindset habits that you can easily practice daily.

- Habit 1—Stillness: The first habit would be to enhance your sense of presence in the moment before you aimlessly scroll or consume information without processing it critically. Start by doing breathing exercises where you focus on your mind through breathing, meditation, or concentration exercises. Starting your day with this habit to bring a sense of calm and focus to your thinking can set your mind up for a healthy day.

- Habit 2—Mental Diet Check/Cognitive Nutrition: Be mindful and strict about the information you consume and assess the sources of this information. Reaching for your phone to scroll through the news headlines as soon as you wake up can leave you feeling overwhelmed or in a negative headspace before you've even started your day. The conscious and deliberate boundaries you set to protect your mental space are the way to strengthen your critical thinking foundation. The information you consume is food your brain will get throughout the day, so make sure it's healthy and stimulating in a good way. It helps to do an audit of the accounts you're following on social media and do your best to replace the fluff with intellectually stimulating materials to expand your growth mindset like audio books and helpful discussions.

- Habit 3—Inquiry: It's impossible and unhealthy to shut yourself off from all sources of information, so encourage yourself to ask questions about the information you choose to consume. Interrogate the sources, the evidence presented, and the alternative perspectives, especially when it comes to news, conversations with friends, and advice you're considering implementing. Being rigorous about questioning information can help you reflect on biases or fallacies you might've missed. This creates room to improve your thinking and lets you think deeper than your immediate emotional responses to information.

- Habit 4—Journaling: Keeping track of your thought processes, thinking habits, biases that crop up, and noting the times you felt overwhelmed or emotionally triggered by information is a helpful source of data to help you improve your critical thinking skills.

Exercise 4: Habit Tracking

Critical thinking is far from a "one size fits all" concept, and each of our lifestyles and challenges is unique. Your version of a healthy mindset, therefore, looks different from someone else's. Start mapping your path to become a stronger thinker by choosing one of the habits mentioned above and committing to it for at least seven days. Keep a visual or written record of how your thoughts, habits, and opinions change as you apply your chosen habit to different situations. For example, you could use your journal to record the questions you ask yourself about two articles or news headlines you come across each day. You could also monitor how you feel after replacing a few humor or news-related accounts on your social media with motivational and informative content. Reflect on your progress after seven days and identify areas for improvement.

Key Takeaways

- Developing your critical thinking skills is like building a house, which starts with choosing the right piece of land and building a strong foundation before filling up the space with the right habits and thinking processes.

- Mental clutter is a common state of mind in the current information overload, and it can leave us feeling overwhelmed as if mental clarity is an impossible destination to reach.

- Decluttering your mind is important for your physical and mental well-being because it can help you make better decisions, develop your intellect, prevent overthinking, and make positive distractions become stimulating hobbies that help you decompress and live a more meaningful and aware life.

- Writing down your thoughts, regularly journaling, spending time in solitude and stillness, helpful inquiry and dialogue, and auditing the information you consume are great ways to silence your noisy thoughts and clear the mental clutter.

In the next chapter, we'll work on increasing your sense of self-awareness by naming, shaming, and eliminating your existing biases, beliefs, and opinions that are standing in the way of improving your critical thinking skill set.

Chapter Two

Know Thyself

Biases, Beliefs, and Blind Spots

The trouble with most folks isn't their ignorance. It's knowing so many things that ain't so.

Josh Billings

I n constructing your critical thinking "house," where the mental de-clutter is finding the perfect piece of land and learning how to use logic to lay a strong foundation for the building, increasing your sense of self-awareness will be like selecting the strongest cement to put the bricks of your thought processes together. Reflecting on your habits, beliefs, and biases by becoming more self-aware will help you become a better analytical and objective thinker, which will help you make clearer decisions. Recognizing your thought patterns and obstacles that might be blocking your path to true objective thinking will drastically improve your critical thinking skills. In this chapter, we'll explore the concept of cognitive biases and how your brain relies on these shortcuts to make decisions that keep you in your thinking comfort zone. We'll delve into how to transform a sense of self-awareness into a tool to help you think more critically and why using your emotions to justify and make decisions is holding you back from taking the reins of decision making in your hand.

Cognitive Bias 101—Your Brain's Shortcuts

Even though our brains are more powerful and sophisticated than the most advanced computers, our human nature makes our brains prefer to process information in the simplest and shortest way possible. These shortcuts our brains use to simplify the processing of information are known as heuristics. The vehicles that help your brain navigate to these shortcuts to help you make decisions are known as cognitive biases. A scenario similar to how your brain uses cognitive biases to simplify and process information is a common one: you get home from work late. You're hungry but too tired to cook something from scratch. You know you have a food delivery app on your phone where you can order fast food that you know will satisfy your hunger, even though you know the fast food you order might not be the healthiest thing you could eat. Choosing to order fast food and giving into that desire for convenience is like leaning into your cognitive biases to help you make decisions when confronted with information to process. Choosing to cook a healthy meal instead because you know it's better for your body in the long term is like using critical thinking to process information because you know it's better for your brain and decisions in the long term.

Cognitive biases result in glitches in your thinking process. They can stem from your upbringing, the information you choose to consume, or from you incorrectly remembering an event, your behavior during that event, and the actual reasons why you made the decision you did during that event. Many cognitive biases also stem from your brain preferring to have selective memory or choosing to pay attention to the information that supports your opinion or beliefs. The danger of relying on cognitive biases is that they (negatively) influence our thinking and present our brains with a blurred perspective of the full picture that favors the shortest and easiest route to a decision. The first hurdle to stopping yourself from relying on your biases to make decisions is recognizing when these biases start to creep in and influence your thinking. The following are the common types of cognitive bias:

- Confirmation Bias: This bias crops up when you pay more attention to information that agrees with your existing beliefs. This bias is like an echo chamber where you believe your thinking is right because you're surrounded by opinions that agree with your own. Calibrating your news feed, friend group, or social media to only include information, stories, and opinions that you agree with is an example of giving in to confirmation bias. Disregarding any opposing views as incorrect or absurd is an example of confirmation bias.

- Anchoring Bias: This bias limits your perspective by making you form an opinion on a topic based on the first sound bite or information you hear or read about a topic. Convincing or skewed statistics about the cost of living or your earning potential can anchor your opinion about that information. Hearing the first price option on something you want to buy can influence you into thinking that this value is what the item is actually worth.

- Hindsight Bias: This is where you believe that you knew how a situation would turn out after the result has materialized. Believing that life is more predictable than it appears is a comforting thought that can influence how you process your past mistakes, regrets, or missed opportunities. Examples of hindsight bias include believing that you knew your favorite team or chosen candidate would win or lose after the fact. An example of this bias is when you review a failed test and believe you really did know the right answers to the questions you answered incorrectly.

- The Halo Effect: This bias involves believing that a person or situation that meets your subjective standard of attractive, correct, or right is essentially good and can't be wrong or flawed. This bias holds onto your first impression of a person or situation and limits your ability to remain objective about them, or it because you've already decided that you're correct. This bias creeps in during the job interview process, where the way you're dressed can influence people as to your competence or intelligence. Political candidates rely on this bias to gain popularity.

- The Sunk Cost Fallacy: This bias involves sticking to a strategy even though it's failing in the hopes of recovering what you've lost. It can creep into work situations where you need to prove yourself and will delay acknowledging that a project isn't working, just because you've invested time and resources into it. This bias tries to work around the difficulty of having to cut your losses by wanting to get out as much as you invested into something.

Exercise 5: Bias Bingo

Training your brain to recognize and avoid leaning into your cognitive biases will increase your self-awareness and help you process and analyze information in a more rational way. The goal of the Bias Bingo exercise is to identify your biases and to actively choose objectivity over the comfort of subjectivity and an echo chamber. For this exercise, you'll need to keep the list of cognitive biases and their brief descriptions nearby over the next few days. Identify at least five of these biases as you go about your day, watch the news, or converse with those around you. Once you've identified your reliance on at least five of the biases, cross them off on the Bias Bingo card (Figure 2) and journal about what brought on your biased thinking and how the bias impacted your decision or thought process.

- Actor-Observer Bias: Believing that your decisions and their consequences are influenced by factors outside of your control, but those of others are influenced by their own actions. Self-serving bias relates to this bias, in that you tend to attribute positive outcomes to your own skills and negative outcomes to factors outside of your skills or knowledge.

- Anchoring Bias: Believing the first bit of information about a topic is the sum of the parts of that topic and ignoring information to the contrary.

- Availability Heuristic: Relying on information that reaches the top of your mind the fastest, regardless of its correctness.

- Confirmation Bias: Seeking out or recognizing information

that agrees with your beliefs and opinions.

- False-Consensus Effect: Believing that others agree with your opinions more than they realistically do.

- Halo Effect: Perceiving a person, topic, opinion, or belief as good or correct because it's attractive to you or aligns with your view.

- Misinformation Effect: Relaying a past event through the lens of your own opinion or perception of that event.

- Optimism/Pessimism Bias: Believing that you're more likely to succeed or fail than those around you based on your emotions or opinions in the moment. This reliance on your emotions to perceive a situation can negatively impact your ability to make a rational decision.

- The Sunk-Cost Fallacy: The inability to move on and cut your losses when a choice you make is having clearly negative outcomes because you've invested so much into your choice.

Actor-Observer Bias	Anchoring Bias	Availability Heuristic
Confirmation Bias	False-Consensus Effect	Halo Effect
Misinformation Effect	Optimism/Pessimism Bias	Sunk-Cost Fallacy

Figure 2: Bias Bingo

Harnessing Self-Awareness as a Superpower

The thought of developing your self-awareness might seem daunting at first because of the possibility of learning things about yourself and your long-held beliefs that you may not like or want to believe. However, the enhanced perspective you'll gain if you work on increasing your self-awareness is invaluable to living a more fulfilled life and making better decisions. Being more self-aware is like being a good driver who observes the rules of the road while making use of every mirror and checking procedures to ensure that you don't miss any blind spots and are aware of your impact on the road. Self-awareness involves more than simply knowing more about yourself, it means paying attention to what you constantly learn about yourself, harnessing your strengths, and working on your areas for improvement by removing or minimizing destructive biases and beliefs that can hinder your ability to think clearly. Self-awareness means being brutally honest and objective with yourself about yourself, your feelings, reactions, thoughts, habits, and behaviors.

In every superhero story, there's a part of the plot that focuses on how that hero comes to grips with their superhuman abilities, accepts them as part of who they are, and works on harnessing them to do good in the world. Harnessing your self-awareness works in the same way, you have to be honest about yourself, accept who you are and your actions, and work towards using what you learn about yourself to become a better person who makes better decisions. Consider The Hulk understanding that getting angry is the way to summon his superpowers, or Superman learning that Earth's yellow sun is what gives him his abilities. Identifying the underlying roots of why you make the choices you've made is key to making clearer decisions. These roots could be positive or negative but simply knowing of their existence and taking action to grapple with them enhances your thinking abilities.

The first step in your superhero training montage to increase your self-awareness is to get to grips with your emotions. Suppressing your emotions and being clinical about how you make decisions will throw your decision-making abilities off kilter. Learning when to trust your brain or your gut is a concept you'll explore in the coming chapters, but overall, you need to acknowledge your feelings about a situation to be more aware of how you're making your decision about it.

The next step to self-awareness is being diligent about tracking your thinking patterns, noting the emotions that flare up when you're faced with a decision to make, and the factors you weigh to make your decision. Writing everything down in a journal or on a vision board can help you identify habits and thinking patterns that you wouldn't normally notice if you kept this information only mentally stored. You can easily identify what to work on and what habits need to be eliminated from your thinking processes. The last step to self-awareness requires you to branch out from tuning into your feelings to tuning into other aspects of your life that affect your thinking. These other factors could include your stress levels, your energy levels, your diet, your social interactions, your career choices, and your hobbies. By tracking these aspects in a written or visual way, you'll be able to identify the motivations behind your thinking and decisions while bringing any problematic beliefs and biases to the foreground to eliminate them.

Exercise 6: What's Driving My Thinking?

Your self-aware superhero persona can be revealed by increasing your understanding of how you see the world and what drives this perspective.

Self-aware individuals are naturally more open to feedback and demonstrate greater cognitive flexibility. Flexibility gives you variety, and variety in thought leads to learning and making well-informed decisions.

For this exercise, reflect on a recent decision that you made. The decision you choose can relate to your personal life and relationships, your career, your finances, or your plans for your future. Take a few minutes to do a "brain dump" regarding the decision and write down the important aspects of it. Next, ask yourself the following questions about this decision:

1. What were my core beliefs or assumptions that drove me to make this decision?

2. Where did those core beliefs or assumptions come from? Did they come from my upbringing, my life experience, or my social and cultural background?

3. Did my emotions influence the outcome and decision in any way?

4. Would someone else who holds different beliefs have made a different choice?

For example, you've made an expensive impulse purchase of a new luxury car or appliance:

1. You made this decision because you believe you deserve a reward for working hard recently, and you assume that most people treat themselves this way. You also believe a new car or appliance improves your lifestyle.

2. Your belief originated from discussions you've had with your family about spoiling yourself because you work hard, or that

your friend group all have the item and you don't want to feel left out.

3. Your emotions influenced your decision because you didn't take time to think the purchase through and relied on your impulses that transformed a "want" into a "need".

4. Someone else who is focused on saving or investing their income, someone who is unable to meet their basic financial needs, or someone who believes that luxury items damage the environment might not have made the same decision.

Relying on external influences, your emotions, and a perceived sense of reward can lead you to make impulsive financial decisions that can sometimes have negative consequences. Catching yourself and stopping yourself before your brain makes decisions on autopilot helps you to build metacognition, or the ability to think about thinking. Self-awareness helps you replace automated thinking with intentional and rational thinking.

Overcoming Emotional Reasoning

Understanding your emotions and what triggers them leads to understanding your thinking patterns and decisions. We're all driven by emotions to act and not act. This makes your emotions valuable signals of your potential behavior or choices, but emotions can also cause your biases to surface, distort your perception of the evidence before you, and lead to poor judgment. Learning to separate your feelings or emotions from the facts or evidence is key in critical thinking. For example, you're in a group of friends who you believe are more intelligent than you, so you start to feel intellectually inadequate. Your emotions trigger you to believe that you're actually inadequate, even though there is no evidence to prove this true. Another example of how your emotions can drive you to using emotional reasoning to make decisions is where feelings of jealousy from seeing your partner talk to someone else leads you to assume that they are being unfaithful to you, despite having no evidence to corroborate this assumption. These examples prove that emotional reasoning is a form of cognitive distortion where your emotional reaction to a situation is used to assume the situation's truth or reality.

Attaching a meaning to every feeling can lead to you drawing conclusions based on these emotions, distort your perception of reality, become mentally overwhelming, and cause bad decisions. The first step to avoiding the hazards of emotional reasoning starts with realizing that emotions are temporary. Internalize this concept and caution yourself about allowing a fleeting feeling to be the unstable steering wheel that you use to navigate through your life decisions. The next step to working through emotional reasoning is to acknowledge your emotions and understand that you can't think critically by ignoring them and making decisions in an emotional vacuum. You need to find a balance by identifying your emotions and the facts of the situation. Objectively assess the situation to find evidence or facts that either justify or disprove your emotions. Once you've distinguished between facts and your feelings, work on your objectivity by mentally removing yourself from the situation and talking to yourself about it as if you would talk to someone you care about to help guide them through it. During this step of self-talk, it's important to not judge yourself or be overly critical about your reactions or decisions because emotions are complex and difficult to control.

Exercise 7: Feelings vs. Facts Table

Distinguishing between facts and feelings is an important tool to help you clarify your thinking processes and remove emotion from your decision-making. The aim of this exercise is to sharpen your ability to separate how you feel about a situation from what's actually true about it. This skill will help you think clearly when under pressure. The next time you're feeling a strong emotional reaction to a situation at work, home, school, or in your daily life, take a beat and complete this simple table (Figure 3). Do this exercise at least once a day for a week or as often as you need to work through your emotions and think more clearly about a situation.

Emotion	Thought Triggered	Fact or Feeling?	Balanced Alternative
E.g. Anxiety	I'm going to mess up my presentation at work.	Feeling	I'm nervous because of the stakes, but I've prepared well.

Figure 3: Feelings vs. Facts

Key Takeaways

In the next chapter, you'll discover the power of asking yourself the right questions to evaluate evidence and distill the truth about any situation you might face. Before you release your inner detective and philosopher, let's recap how knowledge about yourself is true power in the realm of critical thinking:

- Cognitive biases are convenient mental shortcuts that your brain relies on to process information and output a solution or opinion about the information.

- Recognizing and identifying your cognitive biases can help you eliminate them using rationality and objectivity.

- Acknowledging the emotions that impact your thinking is key to becoming more self-aware.

- Emotional reasoning can distort your perception of reality. Overcome emotional reasoning by realizing that emotions are temporary, distinguishing between facts and your feelings, acknowledging your emotions, and understanding that you can't think critically by ignoring them.

Chapter Three

Mastering Inquiry

Questions Are Power

He who asks a question is a fool for five minutes; he who does not ask a question remains a fool forever.

Chinese Proverb

Questions and the art of inquiring about the right things are powerful tools that have helped advance our existence since the beginning of human civilization. The foundations of philosophy, law, medicine, science, politics, and economics lie in the answers to fundamental questions, and new knowledge is only revealed through questioning the existing status quo. Mastering the art of asking the right questions is essential to improve your critical thinking because questions are related to analysis, curiosity, and flexibility, all of which are necessary to think critically. To bring home this seemingly abstract concept of how to ask questions, think back to watching your favorite legal drama or film. Consider that moment when the hotshot lawyer corners the defendant or a key witness on the stand by asking them some difficult questions during a brutal cross-examination. These questions are based on damning evidence and lead to the climax of the plot where the truth is ultimately revealed. This demonstrates the power of questions and how our thinking processes would suffer from a lack of focus without using inquiry. In this chapter, you'll learn how to ask the right questions, when to use open or closed-ended questions, and elevate your sense of curiosity to delve deeper into your thinking process.

The Art of Asking the Right Questions

Teaching yourself how to ask questions to enhance how you think might seem like an abstract concept to grasp. To simplify it, you must look at the root of the purpose of asking questions, which is curiosity. Curiosity and its related needs to seek, discover, and learn are what make us human and keep our minds engaged and active. If you feel you might've lost your sense of curiosity in the midst of the stress of your career and the demands of the world's fast pace, be comforted by the fact that curiosity was the way you learned the fundamentals in your early childhood years. Curiosity is inherent within you; therefore, so is your ability to think critically by using questions to gain knowledge. The importance of nurturing your curiosity and remaining open-minded is essential for your mental and intellectual well-being. Curiosity stimulates your ability to learn and cognitively develop by taking in and interpreting information. A curious brain is more resilient and adaptable in the face of unexpected changes because you'll be able to make clearer decisions. The foundations of innovation lie in creativity, which requires the curiosity to explore uncharted ideas and question accepted norms or solutions.

Just like in your childhood, encouraging curiosity means asking questions. Mastering the skills of asking the right questions can drive clarity and focus in your thinking as you discover new evidence about a situation. AI technology is starting to dominate the world where we have almost unlimited access to information and facts but knowing how to sift through it to find what is relevant, true, and necessary requires you to be strategic about the questions you ask. Making better decisions starts with asking better questions, challenging accepted assumptions, and grappling with your mental blind spots. You can become a strategic interrogator by understanding the five different types of questions: investigative, speculative, productive, interpretive, and subjective (Chevallier, Dalsace, and Barsoux, 2024).

Investigative questions identify what you need and how to go about achieving it. Questions using "how" and "why" are excellent to discover your purpose before solving a problem. For example, you're facing the problem of overspending on your corporate budget. Asking yourself why you need to save funds and how to go about it will reveal solutions. Speculative questions help you see the bigger picture from different angles and prevent a limited perspective when solving a problem. With the budgeting example, you could ask, "What if we explore quotes from different marketing companies to reduce marketing costs?". Productive questions encourage you to look ahead into the practicalities of your solutions. These involve asking yourself "Now what?", or in the budget example, "Now that we've reduced our spending, how do we accurately track our budget to prevent this problem from happening again?".

Interpretive questions digress from the norm but can lead to innovative solutions. These questions require you to make sense of the problem and break it down to its core to determine the effectiveness of your proposed solutions and the consequences. In your budget example, you could ask, "What lessons did we learn from this problem?" or "How was revisiting our budget useful for the team?". Staying true to the purpose of solving the problem is essential to learn and grow from the solution you choose to implement. Subjective questions help you identify your biases, blind spots, emotions, and unsaid intentions when you're trying to solve a problem. Unchecked and unresolved subjectivity can derail the solution you attempt to implement, so these personal issues must be addressed, even if it's uncomfortable to do so. In the budget example, failing to address an issue like budgeting constraints, leading to your team being concerned about their job security, could negatively impact the reduced budget you decided to implement because they're resistant to the budget itself or to offering ideas to reduce it. The above five types of questions should be used in combination when solving a problem or making a decision, but each one must be used when it's strategically helpful to your decision-making process. Learning when to ask each requires practice. You should apply each question to every important decision you make, no matter how low the stakes are. Choosing the right question to ask at the right time can unlock valuable insight into a problem leading you to the best solution.

Exercise 8: Unpacking a Current Challenge

This exercise is intended to help you adopt a questioning or curious mindset instead of being solely focused on reaching a conclusion or solution.

1. Select a current challenge in your life. This could be a decision to make or a problem to solve. It could be related to your career, personal relationships, finances, or your own personal growth.

2. Write down the first five questions about the challenge or problem that come to mind. Work on refining these questions to get to the root of the issue, which will eventually reveal the solution. Base your refined five questions on the five different

question types we explored above.

3. Write down any new information about the challenge that you uncover through asking more probing questions that you didn't know before you began the exercise.

Open vs. Closed Questions—When to Use Each

Questions must be used as tools to gain insight, information, and to assist you in making a decision about the way forward or about the truth. Knowing what type of information you want to learn about a challenge is the first step in knowing what type of questions you want to ask to learn this information. This is where understanding the difference between closed and open-ended questions comes in. Knowing the difference can be likened to fishing in the open ocean. Choosing to ask open-ended questions is like casting out a large fishing net that could catch any type of information, ranging in size and species from shrimp to sharks. Choosing to ask closed-ended questions is like using a fishing pole and a specific bait to catch a specific type of fish. Using each type will impact the evidence or data you're able to gather, which will ultimately affect your final decision.

Open-ended questions encourage discovery, dialogue, creativity, and consideration of different perspectives. These questions ask for opinions, thoughts, feelings, and unique stories about the topic. Open-ended questions can only be answered from your own unique perspective and in your own words. They are usually used when you want to look at a situation from different angles because they are answered by exploring the reasoning or "why" behind an opinion, which is usually based on the personal experience of the person answering. Open-ended questions are usually used in interviews, feedback sessions, or marketing research to gain insight into the mindset of the target group. Examples of open-ended questions in various scenarios include the following:

- Where do you see your career going in the next five years?

- Why did the image used in this advertisement catch your attention?

- How did you benefit from using this product?

- What would improve your experience with us as a customer?

- What do you think about before deciding to make an investment?

Open-ended questions shouldn't lead to only one answer and should be structured in a way that encourages the person answering to open up about their thoughts on a subject. Asking your subject to explain something, to provide an example, to provide their opinion on a topic, or to relay a personal experience on the topic are ways to ask open-ended questions. The risks of only using open-ended questions are that you can get answers that are so broad that the information within them becomes unusable as evidence, and the questions can sometimes fail to bring about any concrete data to weigh the factors required to reach a critically thought-out conclusion. Open-ended questions can also sometimes be prompting the person to give an answer with a specific theme. Be wary of these risks when drafting your open-ended questions.

Close-ended questions are used to get an exact answer, so these are useful to confirm facts (fact-checking) or to narrow down your options. These questions ask for yes or no, or precise answers and lead to the extraction of usable data that can be quantified in charts to lead to important decisions (Katz, 2025). Close-ended questions can be used to learn factual information either about the person being questioned or about the topic in question. These questions are used to set the factual scene of an investigation before open-ended questions are used to determine the reasoning behind the investigation. Close-ended questions should be used when you need accurate and exact answers about facts as data. The risk of using closed-ended questions is that you'll only get one answer to work with, and it will likely be factual and not based on opinion or emotion. Close-ended questions can include those that yield yes or no answers or can be multiple choice, as long as the choices cover the full range of possible outcomes. Always be careful of hiding answers in your close-ended questions. For example, asking "Do you think your colleagues are lazy?" requires a yes or no answer, but an opinion has already been built into the question. Examples of close-ended questions include the following:

- Were you happy with the service you received from our team?

- Are you satisfied with your performance so far at the company?

- Do you have experience in managing a team of more than six people?

- Did the image used in this advertisement catch your attention?

- Do you benefit from using this product?

An example of where close and open-ended questions are used together is any police procedural drama or true crime documentary. Investigators will use closed-ended questions to determine the hard facts of the situation, such as the age, gender, and physical features of the victims and the probable suspect. The open-ended questions will be used to interview witnesses and to determine the suspect's motive for committing the crime. Surveys are another good example of closed and open-ended questions working together to paint a picture of the surveyor's ideal customer, job applicant, or participant. Deciding when to use each type of question depends on your overall goal, i.e., do you want to explore a problem (open-ended) or are you ready to make a decision about a problem (close-ended). Note that one can be used as a precursor to the other when you're problem solving.

Exercise 9: Applying Open and Closed Questioning

Life isn't always black and white, and you might need to apply both open and closed-ended questioning techniques to find a solution to a problem you're currently facing.

1. Consider a recent conversation or decision that you wanted to handle better than you did in the moment, or one that's coming up soon where you have to make a decision. Your chosen scenario could relate to your job, your personal relationships, your finances, or your goals for the future. Let's take the example of wanting to ask your boss for a promotion or a raise.

2. Reconsider three questions you actually asked in this situation, or that you have in mind to ask if it hasn't happened yet. Reconsider these three questions as both open and closed-ended to help expand your critical thinking about this dilemma you have or will face. In our example of asking your boss for a raise or promotion, your questions for yourself or your boss could look something like the following:

   a. Close-ended question 1: Are you satisfied with the revenue

       I've brought in over the financial year?

   b. Open-ended question 1: What more could I have done to bring in revenue over the last financial year?

   c. Close-ended question 2: Have I signed up for any additional training in my field recently?

   d. Open-ended question 2: What are my long-term and short-term goals within the company?

   e. Close-ended question 3: What would I consider a fair promotion/salary increase, and do I have data to justify this request?

   f. Open-ended question 3: Why do you/I feel I deserve a promotion/salary increase?

3. Record your reflections and what you learn by transforming each question from a musing into a tool to gather evidence and information.

How to Drill Deeper with "Why" and "What If"

Getting to the root cause of a challenge or problem is an essential aspect of thinking critically and finding the best solution. As you've now learned, questions are more than empty musings or cries for help in a crisis. Instead, they're tools to be harnessed to find out the right quality and quantity of information you need to reason through a problem. The analogy of drilling deeper to get to the root of a problem makes sense because a miner drills deeper with a goal of finding gold, oil, or diamonds.

You need to drill deeper to find meaning and solutions to the situation you face in life.

Asking yourself "Why?" can lead you down the path of discovery and help you reveal root causes, motivations, and the hidden aspects of a problem. This is the first tool you'll need to break ground on your deeper drill into a problem. Keep asking yourself why until you hit a wall or a light bulb moment. For example, you want to start eating healthier and exercising more regularly. To start your health journey, try out the following question chain:

- Why are you unable to be healthy right now?

  ○ Because you eat fast food at least three times a week. Why?

  ○ Because you're too tired to cook when you get home from work. Why?

  ○ Because you wake up tired and have to get up early for your commute. Why?

  ○ Because you tend to sleep after midnight or work into the late hours of the night at home.

- You've reached the root cause of your unwillingness of cooking yourself healthy meals: your exhaustion stems from sleeping late and not being more strict about a work-life balance or switching off when you get home.

Now that you've broken ground by asking why, move on to asking "What if?" to brainstorm and mentally test out solutions to the problem. You're now thinking outside the box of the problem after naming and shaming it as you narrowed it down with your "Why?" question chain. Asking "What if?" can spark your creativity and sharpen your problem-solving skills by deeply exploring each solution, alternatives, and their likely consequences. Let's apply the power of "What if?" to the example of your desired health journey:

- What if you came home earlier to cook your meals? You can't because your job doesn't have flexible working hours.

- What if you joined a gym and went straight after work? This could help you wind down after work and force you to exercise if it fits into your budget.

- What if you fully or partially prepared your meals on a Sunday afternoon? If you don't have social obligations, you could easily set aside two hours on a Sunday to get this done.

- What if you tried to sleep at the same or similar time every day to ensure you're rested in the morning? It might work, but you don't want to be so rigid during your free time.

Exercise 10: Reflective Questioning

A simple brainstorming session builds on the information gathered from your "Why?" questions and transforms them into solutions using "What if?". Apply the power of this questioning technique to your daily life using the following:

1. Choose a routine, belief, or plan that you routinely follow and rarely question. This exercise will be more effective if you choose a negative routine, belief, or plan that you'd like to reassess and change to improve yourself. Scrolling through your social media before bed or being anxious about new social or

work situations are examples you could use here.

2. Ask yourself, "Why do I do this?" at least three times, where you delve deeper into the problem and your behavior each time to reveal the root cause.

3. Once you've found the root cause, ask "What if I tried something different in this situation next time?" and brainstorm at least three alternatives to your current behavior or belief.

4. Write down your findings after questioning yourself and after implementing the alternative behaviors.

Key Takeaways

You're going to delve deeper into the connection between self-awareness and critical thinking in the next chapter by learning how to put your ego aside in favor of looking at evidence objectively. Before we explore evidence, let's recap what you've learned about how to use questions in critical thinking.

- Questions stem from curiosity, which helps us remain open-minded, open to knowledge, and enhances our ability to look at a problem from various perspectives to yield the best solution.

- Questions are tools that must be used to learn information and gather evidence to help you make a decision.

- Investigative, speculative, productive, interpretive, and subjective questions can be used to discover different aspects of a problem and its potential solutions.

- Open-ended questions must be used to encourage exploration and creativity, and closed-ended questions must be used to provide data or definitive answers.

- Asking "Why?" identifies the root and hidden aspects of a problem, and asking "What if?" allows you to harness your findings to test out possible solutions.

Chapter Four

Evidence Over Ego

Evaluating Information Like a Pro

Do not believe in anything simply because you have heard it. Do not believe in anything simply because it is spoken and rumored by many.

Buddha Siddhartha Gautama Shakyamuni

The term "skeptic" has been historically viewed in a negative light. The word tends to invoke the image of someone who looks for reasons to disagree with accepted norms or one who mistrusts opinions that deviate from their own. However, there's a difference between a skeptic and a cynic. Cynics double down on their beliefs and opinions, even when faced with reliable, contradictory evidence. Skeptics, on the other hand, question, analyze, and seek reliable evidence to determine the truth. Skepticism is important in critical thinking because it requires you to be led to conclusions solely by the evidence and context in front of you, regardless of your opinions about the source of the evidence or your biases or beliefs. Being skeptical about the information you consume is a healthy habit to incorporate into your thinking routine. In this chapter, you'll learn how to distinguish between credible and unreliable evidence, why being skeptical about the source and context of evidence is wise, and how to eliminate your biases and emotional blind spots from your perspective on evidence.

How to Spot Good vs. Bad Evidence

You've likely heard the warning not to believe everything you read or watch. In light of the current information overload we're in, skepticism and questioning supposed evidence that proves things true or false are lifelines you can use to stay true to your critical thinking abilities. Training your brain to discern between good and bad evidence becomes invaluable when navigating the information overload and making decisions in your personal life. At a high level, good evidence comes from reliable sources, is verifiable, and it's relevant and not outdated. Bad evidence is information that can contain facts that have been skewed or manipulated to appeal to your emotions. Bad evidence is often based on personal anecdotes that people use to create a narrative and it lacks credible support. Knowing the difference requires self-awareness and the ability to set aside your personal opinions or biases and remain objective about the credibility of the evidence. Accepting a claim as true without verifying it or at least questioning the credibility of the evidence used to support it puts you at risk of believing and being manipulated by misinformation, which can negatively impact your decision-making abilities.

Credibility means that you're able to trust that the evidence is correct and good. Establishing whether or not you can trust evidence means understanding the three steps you have to take in your analysis to assess whether evidence is good or bad. The first step is identifying the underlying premise, claim, or idea that's being put forward. Consider the example of the weather app on your phone telling you that it's going to rain later in the day. The next step is to assess the credibility of the evidence that supports that claim. You know that the information put forward in your weather app is curated by scientists who are trained in assessing the weather. The app would likely be a failure and not be available on your phone if it was consistently incorrect. The last step is to decide if you can trust the evidence. It is the connection the evidence draws between itself and the initial claim or premise, i.e., you have to ask yourself how the evidence is used as a reason to back the claim. In your weather app example, you can verify the information on the app by checking other weather reports to decide whether or not your weather app's prediction is true. Good evidence is verifiable and can withstand the skeptical test of questioning and fact-checking.

Bad evidence is misinformation disguised as a credible fact, but once you scratch below the surface or personal attachments to it, it tends to lose credibility or be easily disproved. For example, you're scrolling through your social media and come across a fitness influencer who tells you that eating bread is the worst thing you can do for your health. You've been wanting to improve your health, so you pay close attention to their advice and they relay a story of how they and their family members used to eat bread and had to be hospitalized because of the negative impact of bread on their health. If you follow the three steps used to assess evidence with this influencer's advice, you'll start by noting their premise is that eating bread causes poor health. The next step is to assess the credibility of the evidence. Instead of presenting you with studies, scientific data, or different opinions, the influencer told their personal story of how bread put them in the hospital. The last step is to assess how the evidence is used to prove the premise. This influencer is telling you that bread is bad for your health because their family had a negative health experience from eating bread. This evidence isn't credible because it doesn't prove the premise, and it's purely anecdotal or personal without any scientific justification. Bad evidence crumbles under scrutiny and the rigor of skepticism.

Exercise 11: Fact or Fluff?

This exercise will help you stay true to your inner skeptic as you navigate difficult decisions at work, socially, personally, and when you're watching the news.

1. Select a news story or viral claim that's recently been trending in the media. The source could be the mainstream media, or from more alternate sources like social media.

2. Break down the claim made in the story or trend by writing down any evidence you can find to support the underlying premise of the story.

3. Once you have all the evidence in front of you, categorize them into evidence that is "strong," "weak," or "misleading." It also helps to write the source of each piece of evidence as you categorize it.

4. Write down three sentences explaining whether or not you believe the claim made in the story is trustworthy or credible, and the reasons for your opinion.

The Role of Sources, Data, and Context

Critical thinking is an important step on the path to being a better communicator, writer, and thinking reasonably when confronted with conflicting opinions. Using reliable sources, objective data, and taking the context of the evidence into consideration when formulating your opinion on an issue can help you avoid making assumptions about a situation and drawing an incorrect conclusion. Evaluating the source of evidence is key to determining if it's reliable or is mere misinformation. Verify the information you're presented with that is used to prove a claim to be true. Fact-checking has become a double-edged sword in today's technological world because, although it's easier to verify a source of information as credible, it's also easier to be convinced by misinformation. To overcome this challenge, carefully scrutinize the source. Ask yourself if it's a primary source, which is generally the most reliable, or an interpretation or a different version of the evidence provided in a secondary source. Take your analysis a step further by comparing sources and checking if the evidence can be verified by more than one source. The more conflicting evidence you receive or the less of a pattern you see with the evidence, the more likely it is that your source isn't credible. A good example of the importance of sources is in academic writing, where a paper using evidence to prove a claim is peer-reviewed and approved by other people with similar or higher academic qualifications. A source's expertise and reputation can make evidence credible. A source's bias can creep into their perspective of the evidence, and this is important when scrutinizing the source of evidence.

Data and statistics are used as evidence to prove a claim to be true, and we tend to trust them because they're acquired through studies or surveys. The perception is that these are more reliable than mere opinions. However, data and statistics are sometimes cherry-picked to support a specific opinion and present a skewed perspective of the objective facts of a situation. This is why investigating the source from which and the context within which the data was obtained is crucial to deciding whether or not you can trust the data. For example, you see a statistic claiming that 90% of American consumers prefer coffee to soft drinks. Accepting this as true means believing that other drinks are not as popular as coffee. However, a deeper look reveals that the survey that produced the data was done outside a coffee shop on a Monday morning, where 20 consumers out of the 200 seated at the shop were interviewed for the survey. This is a bad or biased sources for the survey because it's likely that those surveyed outside a coffee shop would prefer coffee. A better survey for this group might be a survey on what type of coffee beans they prefer. You have to consider who is making the claim or presenting the evidence, their motivation for doing so, and what information they might be leaving out to sway your opinion. You have to place the evidence or data in its correct context.

The context of the evidence you're analyzing is essential to understanding whether or not you can trust the source and the claim it's allegedly proving true. Consider whether or not the evidence is current or outdated in terms of socio-economic factors, science, morality, the law, and time. For example, blood-letting was considered a sound medical procedure in the past; however, medicine has evolved to prove that bloodletting is a dangerous procedure. Context can help to frame your analysis of evidence and give you insight into the source of the evidence and the reasoning used to bridge the gap between the claim made and the conclusion reached. For example, the reason the United Nations and human rights law were established is because of the atrocities committed during World War II. The amount of checking you should do is based on the claim. For example, if someone said they ate pasta last night, you know that people often eat pasta, and what they ate doesn't affect your life, so you don't need to verify this claim. However, if someone claimed that their neighbor swears that drinking only celery juice for every meal prevents cancer, adopting this habit could affect your life negatively and you would need to do research with medical experts to determine if you should start an all-celery diet. The context sheds light on the evidence and helps you decide if the path to the conclusion makes sense.,

Exercise 12: Source Sleuth

This exercise requires some research into a popular or current story that dominated the news. The objective is to help you build your confidence in evaluating evidence by using critical thinking to determine if it's weak or credible. The exercise should also help you to understand how sources and context influence the credibility of a piece of evidence and how they can be used to distort the facts.

1. Find two news articles covering the same story. These two articles should each be from different news outlets or pages. Finding two new outlets that are opposite in their political views might make the differences more stark and clear.

2. Write down the different ways that each article uses data or statistics and how they each quote their sources.

3. Take special note of differences in which facts are emphasized in each article, the different tone in each, and what context is added or missing from each.

4. Write down your conclusions where you reflect on which article you trust more and why it convinced you that it was reliable evidence of the story.

The Sneaky Trap of Confirmation Bias

Biases are blind spots that can influence not only how evidence is created but also how you decide to process and analyze evidence. Confirmation bias is the most common bias that rears its head in our daily lives because it makes us unconsciously seek out and favor information that supports the beliefs and opinions we already have. Consider the news channels you watch, the brands you purchase, your working style, and your social circle. These aspects of your life are prone to confirmation bias. For example, your colleague is always praised for their performance at work. While out on your lunch break, you see your colleague eating food from a fast-food chain, and you believe that eating fast food is an indisputable sign of poor health and laziness. Your confirmation bias, therefore, led you to assume that your colleague is lazy and unhealthy, despite their good work record. It's important to note that correlating facts does not equal causation, and finding coincidences isn't the same as finding proof. Seeing your colleague eat fast food doesn't prove that they're lazy or unhealthy without the support of credible evidence.

Confirmation bias narrows your perspective and puts your brain in a corner facing the wall, where you ignore any evidence that contradicts your favored beliefs and opinions. This ignorance leaves you with a distorted perception of reality where you're only able to look at the world through your own comfortable lens, instead of actually opening your eyes to possibly being proved wrong or to the benefit of exploring a variety of perspectives. Variety in your thinking routine will only enrich how you think and analyze evidence. Confirmation bias is the result of your brain using its comfortable shortcuts to draw conclusions based on what you selectively expose yourself to, what you choose to pay attention to, and what you choose to remember. Confirmation bias creeps in when you slip into that comfort zone where your beliefs make you feel good about yourself and even superior to others. It can be an unconscious thinking system you fall into, so self-awareness is the best antidote to preventing it from limiting your perspective or unfairly interpreting evidence. Maintain your objectivity, make better decisions, and add color to your thinking routine by consciously exploring opinions and facts that contradict what you believe. Overcome confirmation bias by acknowledging it when it crops up, questioning your beliefs before you make a decision, gathering the objective facts from neutral sources to be objective, and debating your conclusions with others or with yourself to put the evidence and your decisions through a rigorous analysis.

Exercise 13: Belief Buster

The objective of this exercise is to help you identify when confirmation bias crops up in your decision-making processes and how to recognize when it's distorting your thinking method.

1. Choose a belief or opinion you feel passionately about. It could be family-related, work-related, or even political. Write this belief and circle it at the top of your page to make it the center of this exercise.

2. Research credible articles, studies, and opinions that directly oppose your opinion or belief. You might not like what you read, but that's the point of this exercise.

3. Write down the strongest points from the opposing side. Be objective and consider the reasoning and conclusions of the opposing perspective. You're actively training your mind to consider different perspectives. You'll be able to either change your mind or justify your belief strongly based on credible evidence.

4. Reflect on your findings and consider the points from the opposition that surprised you the most or made you reconsider your own beliefs or opinions.

Key Takeaways

The next chapter will involve a deep dive into the practical applications of logic and how to spot fallacies so you can easily identify when things just aren't adding up in an argument or when a claim is being proved with evidence. Before we explore the many facets of logic, let's review the facts we have about evidence:

- Strong evidence is verifiable, relevant, and from reliable sources.

- Weak evidence isn't verifiable, relies on personal stories used to create a perceived narrative, cherry-picked data, and emotional responses.

- Assessing the credibility of evidence requires you to consider the source of the evidence, the method used to obtain the data supporting the evidence, and the context within which the evidence exists.

- Confirmation bias can distort your perception of reality and how you analyze evidence because it makes you favor information that agrees with your beliefs. Self-awareness and exploring opposing opinions are the best way towards objectivity and eliminating confirmation bias.

- Improving your objectivity, considering multiple perspectives, being strict about fact-checking, and acknowledging the flaws in your own thinking process are the best ways to evaluate evidence to help you make sound decisions.

Chapter Five

Logic in Action

Everyday Arguments Decoded

A problem well-stated is a problem half-solved.

Charles Kettering

U sing logic to solve problems is something you might be doing unconsciously, which means it might be a critical thinking skill you already have that's lying dormant without being used to its full potential. Using logic and learning to spot its absence in an argument is key to rounding out your critical thinking method, and it will serve you in solving problems every day. Think back to watching an episode of your favorite police procedural or courtroom drama, or consider the method of the famous fictional detective, Sherlock Holmes. Logic, or the lack thereof, is always used to reach the conclusion of a case based on the evidence and circumstances surrounding that evidence. You'll learn to find your inner detective and debater in this chapter by empowering yourself with practical tools to recognize logical structures and common fallacies, to assess every day simple and complex arguments calmly and critically, and to construct your own logical positions in an argument with confidence and clarity.

Basic Logic and Common Fallacies

Logic is the basic framework we use to assess the structure of arguments or situations. This means that we use our logic to decide if the conclusion drawn from a premise and evidence makes logical sense. Your logic is informed by the evidence, your observations, the context of the premise or claim. Using logic means you're engaging in the act of reasoning through a problem critically. The way you choose to get from the premise to the conclusion, using logic, depends on the type of reasoning or logical framework you choose to adopt. As previously mentioned, the most common methods of reasoning are deductive and inductive reasoning. Knowing when to use either depends on the type of observations and evidence you have available to reason through a problem, and it's important to note that both types of reasoning can be used to make decisions.

Deductive reasoning requires you to start reasoning from a general statement, a widely known premise, or an existing theory, and use logic to analyze the evidence available to draw a specific conclusion that either proves or disproves the initial general statement. Deductive reasoning is a great way to test and prove or disprove a theory. Some deductive reasoning arguments rely on both a major and a minor premise to support the conclusion. For example, the major premise is that all mammals must consume water to live. The minor premise is that dogs require water to live. The conclusion is that all dogs are mammals. A practical example of when to use deductive reasoning would be to decide on a marketing strategy. For example, your general statement could be that all customers enjoy reading social media posts about products they regularly buy. Your next deductive step would be to put forward the theory that your company's customers enjoy reading social media posts about your company's products. You would then assess and analyze the evidence used to support your claim. This evidence could be in the form of the number of followers your company's social media account has or the level of engagement on certain types of posts. If the numbers show that followers or engagement increase the more you post then you can conclude that your customers enjoy reading and viewing social media posts about your company's products. Deductive reasoning is based on an existing certainty and requires you to move from a general claim to a specific conclusion.

Inductive reasoning requires you to start reasoning from a specific statement or claim and use logic to draw a general conclusion, theory, or statement from that specific premise. Inductive reasoning is a great way to use patterns and recurring observations to create a theory. A practical example of when to use inductive reasoning would be to decide on how to organize a brainstorming session or workshop. For example, your specific observations could be that your colleagues tend to feel refreshed when they arrive in the morning, and their attention tends to be more inconsistent after they return from lunch. To test your observations or find a trend, you could observe the energy levels of your colleagues in other meetings leading up to the workshop. Based on your evidence, you could decide to organize future workshops with these colleagues with deep work in the mornings and administrative or more casual tasks in the afternoon. Inductive reasoning is based on an existing probability and requires you to move from a specific claim to a general conclusion. You'll often start out solving a problem using inductive reasoning by turning your specific observations into a claim to prove. Once you've proved those specific observations to be true, you'll use deductive reasoning to either validate or disprove your general premise.

In the abstract, reasoning seems to be infallible and easy to apply; however, just like how your biases can creep in and tint the lens through which you analyze evidence, fallacies can exist within arguments that seem logical without a deeper look. Learning how to identify and dismiss arguments based on logical fallacies will help you champion reason throughout your critical thinking journey. Reason is the arch-nemesis of the logical fallacy, so let's unpack a few types of common logical flaws that come up in heated debates or even when you reason through a situation mentally (Kramer, 2023):

1. Straw man argument: This fallacy relies on creating an exaggerated version of your opponent's premise and/or conclusion instead of grappling with their actual argument. For example, misconstruing your friend's preference for waffles as equating to them having a deep dislike for pancakes.

2. Ad hominem fallacy: Relying on this flaw means dismissing your opponent's argument based on your opponent's personality or a random fact about them. For example, refusing to vote for a political candidate because of the clothes they wear instead of based on their policies.

3. Slippery slope fallacy: This fallacy incorrectly relies on a specific or anecdotal series of events as evidence to support a claim, generalization, or a negative chain of events. For example, suggesting that allowing students to wear colorful t-shirts to school will lead to students losing respect for teachers at school and to them wearing inappropriate clothing.

4. False dilemma: This fallacy presents only 2 choices or options in an argument, which are on the extreme opposites of the spectrum of the situation. Relying on this presentation of a false dichotomy means being deliberately ignorant of any other reasonable option that doesn't fall into the "either/or" presented. For example, claiming that someone who doesn't agree with every government policy is an anarchist who rejects authority and order.

5. Red herring: This fallacy occurs when a point or fact that is irrelevant to the argument is put forward to throw your opponent off. For example, a child uses their chores as a reason to justify the fact that they failed a test at school.

Exercise 14: Fallacy Hunt

Training your brain to recognize logical fallacies and work through them using pure reasoning is the way to think, write, and communicate in a clearer way. Knowing that you've covered your bases in an argument and relied on reasoning instead of emotions or biases to solve a problem will help you develop intellectually and make sound choices in life. This exercise demonstrates how logical fallacies can crop up in your daily life and how to use reason to combat them.

1. Scroll through your news feed or YouTube feed and watch a 5-minute clip from a debate, talk show, or podcast on a topic that interests you.

2. Identify at least two logical fallacies used to further arguments in the debate, regardless of which side you agree with.

3. Describe these logical fallacies in detail in your journal, and what evidence or illogical points are used to support them.

4. Write down what a stronger argument would look like to make the same points made using the logical fallacies.

5. As a bonus exercise, scroll through the comments section of a trending and polarizing social media post and repeat the exercise to hunt down logical fallacies and explore stronger alternatives.

Deconstructing Arguments (Without Getting Heated)

An argument is an "act of expressing a point of view on a subject and supporting that view using such as research, statistics, and examples" (Indeed Editorial Team, 2025). An argument is essentially a claim supported by research and evidence, not a battle to attack the other side until you win the most points raised. The depiction of debate in popular culture and the polarization and politicization of so many aspects of our lives have contributed to the misconception that every issue presents a debate to be won by becoming hostile or attacking the opposing side. However, the true technique of argument is about properly supporting your claims with evidence and reason. The true victory in argument is finding the certain or most probable truth, not the elusive concept of "winning".

A good argument is systematic and able to withstand rigorous scrutiny by your opponent's strongest evidence to the contrary. To present a solid argument, you have to be familiar with the many parts that make up a good argument, starting with your premise or claim and conclusion.

Just like before you set out to travel, you need to know your starting point (premise) and your destination (conclusion). The premise and conclusion are the core of any argument. Knowing the steps you need to take to reach your destination (gathering and analysis of evidence) is how you reach it safely. Just like planning a trip, you have to consider alternative perspectives to your conclusion. This variety in thought can help you eliminate emotion and biases from your arguments.

While the topic of an argument might trigger your emotions and call up your biases to guide your thinking, it's essential that you train your mind to favor logic, evidence, and reason in these heated moments. You can do this by practicing active listening, where you pay attention to the other person in terms of what they say and their body language, and avoid interrupting them, instead of just listening to reply or rebut their points to push yours forward. You can keep a cool head during an argument by clarifying any assumptions you think your opponent might be making. Use questions like "What evidence supports this?" or "What do you mean by that?". Asking clarifying questions encourages discussion instead of causing the other person to stonewall you or get defensive by seeing your questions as an attack. It can be challenging to remain calm and cool-headed during an argument, especially when you have a personal connection to the topic or you strongly believe you're right, but favoring logic, evidence, and reason will always be the better option because this is how you find the truth or solution.

Exercise 15: Cool-Headed Breakdown

Before you dive into any argument, remember that it's an argument, not a battle. You need to find the core premise and conclusion of the argument being proposed. Remain calm and avoid attacking your opponent or relying on your own defensiveness to take your argument further. Winning isn't the point; instead, it should be about finding the truth or reaching a solution based on reliable evidence and reason. This exercise will help you keep your cool during an argument instead of defaulting to a comfort zone of emotional responses and biases.

1. Reflect on a recent disagreement you had with someone, or a disagreement that you observed. It could have occurred at work, in your personal life, or in your group of friends.

2. Write down the main claim or premise and conclusion of the argument, and the points or evidence used to support the journey of reason to get from the premise to the conclusion.

3. Identify any emotional triggers or biases that cropped up during the argument for you or your opponent, and why these triggers or biases might've appeared during the argument.

4. Reconstruct the argument without the reliance on emotions and biases. Focus on the evidence used and whether this actually proves that the premise leads to the conclusion. In your reconstruction, focus on understanding, calmness, and clarity.

How to Build Your Own Logical Case

The direction and depth of your argument depend on the audience you're presenting it to and the type of evidence you have available to prove your claim and conclusion. Whether it's proving to your friends why you love a certain movie that they all dislike, justifying why you deserve a salary increase, or discussing which school to send your children to with your spouse, there are fundamental elements that you must include in every argument to make sure it can withstand probing by an opponent.

Before you present your argument to others, first identify the core of your argument. This core can be the main premise or the conclusion that you need to support. This will help you decide whether you need to use deductive or inductive reasoning. Next, gather relevant and credible evidence to support your claim. Be aware of your biases and emotional responses to either favoring information that supports your argument or unjustifiably dismissing evidence that opposes your points. When gathering evidence, consider evidence and claims that contradict your own and assess the credibility of these counterarguments. Considering these opposing views makes your argument stronger because you have a 360-degree perspective of the issue. Next, develop additional or minor claims that contribute to proving the main claim and conclusion based on the evidence you've gathered. These minor claims must be based on logic and truth. Next, scrutinize your evidence, premises, and conclusion with an eagle eye to pick out biases, logical fallacies, and problematic evidence to ensure that there are no reasoning errors that will weaken your argument. Lastly, it's time to structure your argument to present it to an audience or opponent.

The structure of the argument you present must have a logical flow to clearly indicate how your evidence and analysis get you from your claims to your conclusion. When presenting, start by introducing the problem lying at the core of your argument. For example, you could be presenting an argument about how a drop in sales at your company is because of a recently reduced marketing budget. Keep the introduction to your premise or problem simple and relevant for your audience. Provide enough context to help them see why this is a viable premise and give a brief overview of the evidence you'll be diving into later. Next, present your premise or claim to give them the lens or perspective through which they should view the rest of the argument you present. In the sales and marketing example, the audience must know that you're going to try to prove that the marketing budget is the main reason why sales have declined. Next, present the evidence you gathered and vetted to support your claim. Here you should present the results of studies, statistics, and surveys that validate your claim. This part of your argument must be based on pure fact instead of personal stories or cherry-picked data. In your example, you could show charts depicting sales statistics before and after the marketing budget was cut.

The next step is to show that you've considered all angles of the problem by discussing opposing perspectives and evidence. Work on disproving or discrediting evidence that opposes your claim using analysis instead of emotion. This will establish your argument as objective and strong in the face of disagreement. In the sales example, you could explore other possible causes for the decline in revenue besides the marketing budget. Lastly, state your claim again, sum up the evidence used to prove it, and state how your conclusion is the most reasonable and true among all other possibilities. Relating your conclusion to your audience is a great way to drive home your conclusion and further validate your claim. In your example, stating how a lack of marketing prevents your sales team from reaching your potential customers is a way to cement your claim in the minds of your audience, in combination with the factual evidence presented.

Exercise 16: Build Your Case

Building logical and properly supported arguments is a critical thinking skill that will serve you in your career because it shows you're systematic and will leave no stone unturned in a crisis. In your personal life, it will help you become a better communicator and resist the urge to get personal and emotional when faced with a problem that is uncomfortable or stressful to solve. This exercise brings home the concept of arguing a premise within a critical thinking framework.

1. Choose a topic or issue that you're passionate about. It could be an issue at your current job, within your social circle, or a policy issue.

2. Write down a short and logical argument about a point relating to your chosen issue. Your argument should be five or six sentences long and include the following sub-categories:

   a. A clear claim or premise.

   b. At least two reasons or pieces of evidence that support your claim.

   c. Consider any biases, logical fallacies, or emotional perspectives you might've considered as you researched evidence to support your claim.

   d. A common counterargument to your premise and your reasoned response to it.

   e. Your ultimate conclusion as to why your premise is true or the best solution.

3. Call a friend or colleague and present your argument to them using the structure outlined above and ask them if it makes sense to them or if there are any flaws to your argument they can spot.

Key Takeaways

We're taking your critical thinking one layer deeper by exploring how to structure your thinking into systems in the next chapter. Before we build on the already strong foundation you've created to think critically, let's recap what you've learned about logic and the structure of arguments:

- Logic is the framework you use to decide if the conclusion drawn from a premise and evidence makes logical sense.

- Logic relies on reasoning. Deductive reasoning is based on an existing certainty and requires you to move from a general claim to a specific conclusion. Inductive reasoning is based on an existing probability and requires you to move from a specific claim to a general conclusion.

- Logical fallacies are flaws that are inherent in an argument that remove the reason and sense from that argument.

- Active listening, removing emotion, and focusing on understanding instead of attacking are ways to approach an argument calmly.

- Structuring a good argument requires identifying the core claim and conclusion, supporting your claim with reliable evidence, considering alternatives, and restating why your claim proves your conclusion based on the evidence.

Chapter Six

Thinking in Systems

Seeing the Bigger Picture

If I had an hour to solve a problem I'd spend 55 minutes thinking about the problem and 5 minutes thinking about solutions.

Albert Einstein

G aining clarity in any situation means clearing out the clutter, editing what you need, and organizing the things you need into an ordered and convenient structure or "system". Consider decluttering your closet or refrigerator. You start by removing everything, keeping things you want and discarding things you don't, and then you organize the things you've kept into an accessible system that you'll need to function every day. Your thinking can be ordered in a similar way by adopting the concept of "systems thinking" into your critical thinking routine. Systems thinking is a dynamic way to approach problem solving. It's an abstract concept that can be difficult to grasp; however, once you master it by practicing how to apply it, you'll have a big-picture or bird's eye view of how a problem connects to the aspects of your thinking system that can help you solve it. In this chapter, you'll be introduced to the concept of systems thinking and learn how understanding interconnected parts, patterns, and feedback loops can help you analyze complex problems and make more intuitive and informed decisions with long-term benefits.

Introduction to Systems Thinking

In terms of critical thinking, a system is an "interconnecting network of parts that work together" (Milberg, 2016). Systems thinking requires you to understand that the world is made up of multiple systems which are organized in a hierarchical structure, but they all connect to each other. This means that when a problem comes up to be solved, traditional thinkers see this problem as an isolated anomaly that needs to be solved. A systems thinker, however, sees this problem as a broken part of a bigger system. This problem can cause ripple effects in the overall system because each part of the system depends on the other for the system to function properly. Therefore, systems thinking means realizing, even if a problem is simple, it exists within a more complex system. An example of where systems thinking is used is by medical practitioners. A doctor or nurse understands that the human body is a system made up of different components that rely on each other to help the body function properly. They understand that treating a problem in one part of the body can have a ripple effect on another part, and they will consider this before providing a diagnosis and starting treatment. Systems thinking can therefore help you get a bird's eye view of the bigger picture of the system as a whole while allowing you to delve into the detail of the part of the system causing the problem.

The elements of systems thinking make it a game changer in terms of problem solving through critical thinking because you train your brain to see the impacts of the problem and solution holistically instead of in isolation. You'll be able to solve problems sustainably instead of just for the short-term. The first element of systems thinking is the concept that every system has emergent properties. These are the features the system displays when it's functioning correctly and complete. Let's take the example of a car, which has multiple components that all need to function for the car to work. If the components are in working order and a driver switches on the ignition, the emergent properties of the car will be present as the car moves and provides the driver with transportation. The next element of systems thinking is to understand that all systems exist within a hierarchy while being interconnected. The position of each system in this hierarchy depends on a system's emergent properties. In the car example, the emergent properties of the systems of ride sharing apps depends on there being working cars on the roads. Therefore, the system of working cars is higher in the hierarchy than that of ride-sharing apps, even though these systems are interconnected. The last element of systems thinking is control because decisions must be made to control the system and ensure that it fulfills its purpose within the structure of the world. Control measures how effective and useful a system is. In the car example, the control elements of the system would be having to pass a driver's license test, certify your car is road-worthy, and observe the rules of the road.

Solving a problem using systems thinking means analyzing the dynamics of a system by looking at how each of its components work, synthesizing this information to understand the system's hierarchy or place in the bigger picture, and making decisions within this context to find a solution to the problem. By adopting this holistic approach, you're able to assess the ripple effect of a problem with one component of the system on the entire system and other systems that it's connected to. For example, a car with faulty brakes disrupts the functioning of the car's system and poses a danger to other cars on the road if driven. It's therefore best to use systems thinking to diagnose and solve problems that are important, chronically occurring, familiar, and where there have been unsuccessful attempts to solve previously (Goodman, 2018).

Practically applying systems thinking, delving into the crevices of a problem, and its potential impact if it's not solved. It's essential to search for events, structure, and patterns surrounding the problem to give you the context of the systems it operates within and impacts (Goodman, 2018). Get a variety of perspectives about the problem instead of leaning into assumptions or blaming one person or component of the system for causing the problem. Encourage discussion about the system, its components, and its hierarchy within the context of other systems connected to it because discussion leads to questions and inquiry about the problem. Your discussions and questions should encourage a feedback loop about the problem, where you use the outputs received and outcomes achieved from a discussion about the problem as input for solutions to the problem and preventing it from recurring in the future. Using feedback loops in systems thinking can keep your solutions related to the problem and sustainable in the long-term. For example, your family has frequent conflicts about household chores and responsibilities. Instead of blaming each other for neglecting tasks, you could re-evaluate the system your family uses to assign chores, communication expectations, and recognition. You discuss the issue openly as a family, and you uncover a lack of clarity and communication in chore distribution. Establishing clear expectations, sharing responsibilities, and weekly check-ins creates a sustainable feedback loop that minimizes conflicts and enhances family harmony.

Exercise 17: Map the System

Grasping the abstract concept of systems thinking means implementing it in its simplest form in your daily life. The objective of this exercise is to "map out" a system that's familiar to you to identify its components and observe the interconnection between different systems within your daily life.

1. Choose a familiar system that helps you function in your daily life. It could be your morning routine, how you structure your workday, or your weekend routine.

2. Identify at least five components of that system and draw arrows between them to indicate how they connect to each other. Let's take your morning routine, for example:

   a. waking up late → skipping breakfast → having low energy throughout the day → performing poorly at work due to fatigue → feeling stressed because of your poor performance → struggling to fall asleep due to stress → waking up late again.

3. Identify the problem(s) with each component and use a feedback loop to work on finding solutions.

Cause and Effect—Beyond the Obvious

Identifying the potential impact of a problem within a system leads you to diagnose the problem and find its root cause. Conducting a root cause analysis requires analyzing a problem deeper than its superficial impacts, and it also enables you to observe the problem's actual and potential effects on the system. Aspects of a problem that appear to be the cause might only be a symptom that indicates a deeper pattern of problems to be solved. The effects of a problem can manifest much later after you've identified the cause, but being a proficient problem solver means diagnosing the problem and finding solutions that will prevent the problem from occurring again. Thinking about a problem as linear, too literal, or only superficial, based on what you observed, is an obstacle to expanding your critical thinking and can lead to consequences that you might've overlooked without doing a deeper analysis of the problem.

The goal of conducting a root cause analysis is to find the cause of the problem, solve it, and prevent it from recurring (Traeger, 2025). Learning how to analyze problems will help you become better at your job, improve your communication skills in your personal life, and help you handle stressful situations rationally. Establishing an accurate connection between a problem's root and its actual or potential effects leads you to the best possible solutions that you can tailor to that specific problem. A problem's root and its effect are not always obvious and can be difficult to pinpoint, depending on the information you have about the problem. For example, it's Wednesday and you start to experience a sore and scratchy throat and flu-like symptoms. Instead of searching the internet for your symptoms and stressing yourself out even more, you retrace your steps and remember you met a friend over the past weekend who had the flu. The cause of your sickness was your contact with an infected person. The effects are your current symptoms, having to take a sick day off work, seeking medical attention from your doctor, taking medication, and potentially infecting the people you live with. This example shows that identifying and analyzing the cause and effects of a problem requires deeper scrutiny than your initial observations.

Exercise 18: The Five Whys

The Five Whys is a technique used to deep dive into a problem, its root causes, and its effects. It functions similarly to the feedback loop discussed above, where the outputs of one question are used as the input for the next question, and so on. This problem analysis technique can help you holistically and deeply understand a problem, assess its impact, and create customized solutions to solve the problem for the long-term. The technique helps you peel back the layers of symptoms crowding the problem's root cause.

1. Write down a recurring problem you're experiencing in your career, personal life, or relationships. Let's take the example of constantly missing your deadlines at work.

2. Ask yourself "Why?" five times to dig deeper into the problem, using the answer to the previous question to form the next question. For example:

   a. Why am I missing my deadlines? Because I don't have enough time in the day to complete my work.

   b. Why don't I have enough time in the day to complete my work? Because I find myself helping other people with urgent matters that they place on my desk.

   c. Why do I help other people instead of completing my work first? I find it difficult to say no to my colleagues.

   d. Why can I not say no to my colleagues? Because I want them to like me and see me as a good person.

e. Why do I want them to like me and see me as a good person? Because I find it difficult to separate my sense of self-worth from my ability to execute tasks at work.

3. Reflect on potential solutions to the problem you've analyzed. In this case, it would be putting in stricter boundaries so that you can add more structure to your workday and produce good work that builds you a good reputation and speaks for itself.

Making Sense of Complex Problems

Deciding on your problem solving strategy depends on the amount and type of information and evidence available for you to analyze and the type of system the problem sits within. Using systems thinking as your strategy to solve problems equips you to untangle complicated issues and find leverage points where implementing small changes can make a big difference in the long-term. Before you start your problem analysis, understand the components of the system within which the problem exists and look for patterns instead of isolated events caused by the problem.

Let's unpack how to solve a problem using what you've learned about systems thinking and cause and effect analysis. The first step is to define the problem because naming the problem will help you shame it by identifying its roots, and this will eventually lead to your solution. It's useful to consider different perspectives and definitions when defining the problem because you might be subjective or allowing your biases to creep in without hearing from others impacted by the problem. Hearing from others can help you identify aspects and effects of the problem you might've missed. You don't want to end up with the solution to solve for y when you need to actually solve for x. The next step is to identify the root cause of the problem. The Five Whys technique should be applied here to strip the problem down to its bare bones. You might need to consult others at this point to get their observations and objective perspectives on the problem and the answers to your Five Whys questions.

Next, determine who or what the problem affects. This step will give you a clearer idea of the system the problem is malfunctioning within. Identifying those who have a stake in having the problem solved will speak to your solution, assessing how feasible it would be to implement, and whether it will be helpful and sustainable. The final step of solving a complex problem is to define the parameters of your solution. This helps you easily eliminate solutions that are unfeasible based on the previous steps you've taken to get to the solution stage. For example, if you want to get fit and you're a beginner, your solution wouldn't be to start lifting the heaviest weights because this would be beyond your physical parameters at that stage. Your options for solutions can be restricted by financial, political, or technical factors, which must be considered before implementation. Take a beat to consider the impact your solution to the problem could have a week, a month, and year into implementation at this stage.

Exercise 19: Spotting Patterns and Hunting for Leverage

Training your brain to identify patterns can help you identify areas where you can improve an already functioning system or prevent a potential problem from cropping up in the near future. Spotting patterns and areas to leverage improvements or solutions is crucial for critical thinking because it helps your brain avoid those convenient biases and mental shortcuts by favoring a holistic view of a situation. You won't see problems as personal burdens, but rather as system malfunctions to fix. The objective of this exercise is to understand the relation between identifying patterns and solutions to problems.

1. Write down a complex issue that you're passionate about. For example, burnout at work, your health, or your career trajectory.

2. Write down three patterns that you observe that relate to this issue over the next two weeks. The patterns could include you not taking breaks at work, leaving work late, working when you get home, working over the weekends, or not knowing what to do during the little downtime you get.

3. Identify a minimal effort action or change that you can implement almost immediately that could influence the system which you've identified the problem within. For example, try taking a 30-minute lunch break during your workday, or putting your laptop in your closet as soon as you get home from work.

4. Reflect on the change or solution you've implemented into the system. Ask yourself if carving out 30 minutes out of your day is a leverage point for further and more sustainable improvement to your work system. Ask yourself how this solution could potentially have a ripple effect throughout the system. You could improve your physical and mental health and develop a better work-life balance in the long-term.

Key Takeaways

Decision-making and its complicated aspects are the focus of the next chapter, so that you can implement the techniques and thinking routines you've picked up along the way so far. Let's recap what you've revealed about systems thinking and problem solving:

- Systems thinking requires you to understand that the world is made up of multiple systems which are organized in a hierarchical structure, but they all connect to each other.

- A systems thinker sees problems as broken parts of a bigger system and understands that the problem can cause ripple effects in the overall system, because each part of the system depends on the other for the system to function properly.

- Finding the root cause of a problem means peeling back the layers of symptoms surrounding the root to reveal it and the problem's effect, if left unsolved.

- Solving complex problems requires you to define the problem, find its root cause, determine who and what the problem affects, and tailor your solutions to the problem based on your findings.

Chapter Seven

Decisions, Decisions

Tools for Smart Choices

The measure of success is not whether you have a tough problem to deal with, but whether it is the same problem you had last year.

John Foster Dulles

E xploring the different aspects of critical thinking can lead to either an overhaul or modification of your current thinking routine. The concepts and processes we've discussed so far are essential to the critical thinking process and will inevitably broaden your thinking horizons. However, it's important to bring these concepts back home and bear in mind that, most of the time, the point of thinking critically is to make a decision or reach a solution to a problem. Your solution or decision shouldn't be the sole focus of your thinking process, but it's often the goal of following the critical thinking process. In this context, the critical thinking process can be likened to following a recipe for a new dish you want to try, putting your own spin on it, and adapting with the ingredients you have available. The decision or solution you eventually reach is like the final dish that is the result of your hard work in the kitchen. Just like producing a delicious dish, making decisions can be overwhelming and difficult without a framework to refer to. In this chapter, you'll explore how to reach decisions using critical thinking by unpacking the parts of the decision-making process, learning how to use different decision-making tools, and judging when to apply logic or use your gut.

The Decision-Making Process Made Simple

Learning how to evaluate your options and make confident, informed decisions requires you to be aware that there are various structures, models, and methods that you can use to make a decision. However, the foundation of most of the popular decision-making frameworks is the basic decision-making process. The 7-step process works hand-in-hand with the critical thinking process to tie up any loose ends that may have been created during your initial investigation of a problem. As you read on, think about this process like a ladder with rungs or a mountain climb with checkpoints along the way. Implementing the decision-making process helps your brain organize the information about the problem in a deliberate and productive way to lead you to the best solution. To illustrate the application of each step, we'll use the example of you deciding how to pay off your debt in the best way that works with your monthly budget.

Step 1: Define the decision you need to make. Do this by identifying the problem that needs to be solved, the overall goal you'll achieve by making this decision, and how you plan to keep track of the impact of your decision. Being goal-oriented at the start will motivate you to explore every aspect of your decision to achieve your goal. In our example, the decision is how to pay off your debt. The problem is that your debt is delaying your financial goals, which are to be debt-free and to start investing and growing your income for long-term financial security. Measuring the success of your decision means paying your debt off as soon as possible in a way that causes minimal stress to you.

Step 2: Gather evidence and information to ensure that your end result is an informed decision. This step relates closely to critical thinking in that you need to practice self-awareness by looking internally at your own habits and beliefs about your decision, and you need to investigate other perspectives by looking externally to gain objectivity about your situation. Investigation and evidence will give you the most dynamic solution. In the debt repayment example, you'd need to sit down and map out each of your debts, their relevant interest rates, and how long you have to repay them. You'll have to look at this alongside your budget and spending habits to figure out where your leverage points are to pay them off quicker. Externally, you could seek advice from financial experts about the smartest way to repay each debt.

Step 3: Investigate different potential solutions to your problems. These become your decision options. The work you've done in step 1 to identify your overall goal—you'll achieve by making the decision—is your North Star that will guide you to deciding on the best solution. This step is where creativity and asking "What if?" is important because you want to delve into the consequences of going with the different solutions available. In repaying your debt, you could opt for just paying the minimum amount to each debt each month and eventually pay them off within the time given. Alternatively, you could adopt the "avalanche method," where you aggressively throw more money at the debt with the largest interest rate while paying the minimum amounts towards the others. You could also opt for the "snowball method," where you pay off the smallest debt amount first, then use that repayment amount to tackle the next, and so on. Always have more than two solution options so that you don't fall into a false dichotomy situation.

Step 4: Evaluate and weigh the information you've collected in the previous steps. Keep your goal as your guiding light and build up your plan of implementing your solutions around your goal. This step might require tools like a SWOT analysis or decision matrix, which we'll explore later. Consider whether your goal would actually be reached through each alternate solution. The easiest path isn't always the best long-term solution. For example, you could consider taking out a loan to pay off all your debts instantly; however, you'd just be deeper in debt. Paying off the smaller debts first might be more motivating and budget-friendly for you. It will help prevent you from being in debt again in the future, thereby achieving your goal of financial security. At this step, you should rank your solutions in order of how effective they'd be in achieving your goal.

Step 5: Choose a solution to implement. Here you'll consider how this decision will impact your goal in the short-term and long-term. You might even end up combining different parts of the alternative solutions you've investigated to tailor your ultimate decision directly to the problem and your goals. For example, you might decide to implement the avalanche debt repayment method for six months of the year and then switch over to the snowball method for six months, depending on your end-of-year expenses.

Step 6: Implement your solution and track the progress towards solving the problem or reaching your goals. Taking action on your decision can be one of the most daunting steps but always bear in mind that you've done a rigorous investigation in the previous steps to reach this point in the process, so trust yourself and move forward with confidence.

In the debt repayment example, this is when you'd start making payments according to your decided strategy and monitor how much you still owe while staying within your monthly budget.

Step 7: Review and reflect on the impact of your decision against your goal and determine whether or not your chosen solution has solved the problem. It's safer to be holistic in your review so that you consider the positive and negative impacts of your decision and have a view of how it worked in the bigger picture, instead of getting caught up in the details. For example, if your chosen method of debt repayment made you budget so tightly that you weren't prepared for an emergency, you might need to pivot. Reviewing your decision helps you remain agile and adaptable in your thinking and allows you to turn past mistakes into future successes.

Exercise 20: The "One Big Choice" Breakdown

It's difficult to apply the steps of the decision-making process when you're stressed, under pressure, or emotionally overwhelmed about a decision. Give yourself practice by applying it to smaller or less important decisions before building up to the more significant decisions you'll need to make in your career or personal life. The objective of this exercise is to practically apply the decision-making process to your own life.

1. Pick a recent decision you've made in the past. It can be a major or minor decision.

2. Use the 7-step decision-making process to work through your decision by writing down:

    a. The decision you needed to make and your goal.

    b. The information about it that you had access to.

c. The solutions to the problem or the decisions you had to make.

d. The pros and cons of each decision.

e. Your final choice of solution.

f. How did you implement your choice.

g. A reflection of what you'd do differently to make that decision now.

Decision Trees, Matrices, and Models

Using tried and tested tools to supplement your decision-making process can help you feel less anxious and overwhelmed about making hard decisions by preventing decision fatigue. Applying tools like a decision tree, decision matrix, or the SWOT analysis model can help you turn vague choices or solutions into structured and solvable problems. Clarity is the goal in critical thinking, and the tools we're about to unpack can make your options clearer.

A decision tree (Figure 4) can be used to help you structure your thoughts relating to a decision and presents a helpful visual of your decision, options, and consequences of choosing those options. A decision tree consists of your decision (the root), branches that represent the path you choose at each step of the decision-making process, and nodes. Making a choice and following a branch leads you to different nodes in the tree. These nodes are the alternative choices that will determine the path that lead to the consequences of your decision. For example, your root or decision is how to tackle your debt. The first alternatives or nodes that would branch out from the root are the snowball or avalanche methods of debt repayment. The next two sets of branches would be at the same level and relate to what action you'll take to pay off your debt with each method. If you choose the snowball method, the first node from the branches connected to this option would be to pay off your smallest debt first, and the second node would be to pay the minimum towards the others. If you choose the avalanche method, the first node from the branches connected to this option would be to pay off your highest interest debt first, and the second node would be to pay the minimum towards the others. The leaves of the tree would stem from these branches of nodes or alternatives and contain the consequences of your choice. Decision trees help you map out consequences and chain reactions visually.

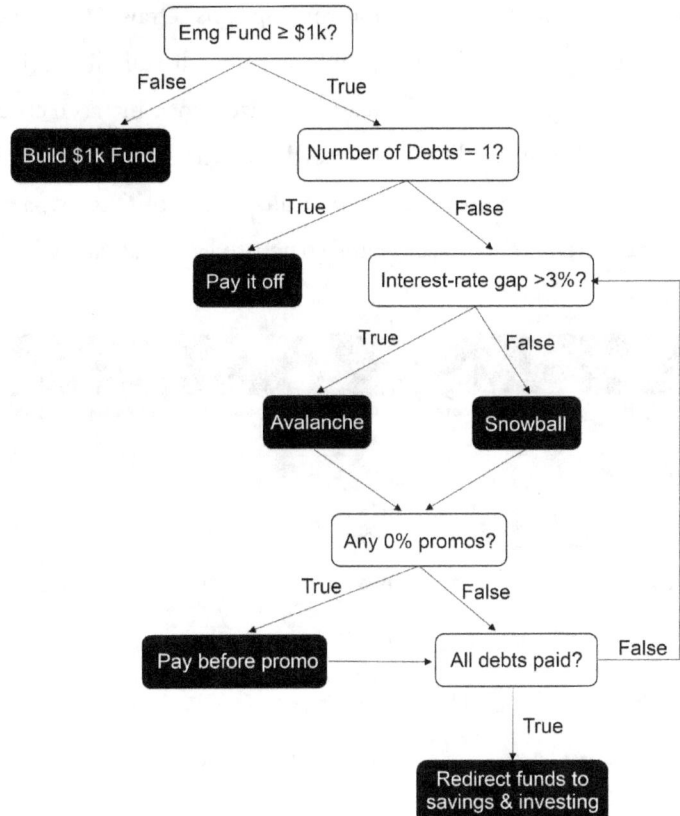

Figure 4: Decision Tree

A decision matrix (Figure 5) helps you evaluate and rank your possible solutions using criteria that you rate your options against. Decision matrices help you narrow your alternatives down to one option when you've already shortlisted alternatives and need to make a final decision, and when you have clear criteria against which to evaluate your options. Create your decision matrix by clarifying the criteria you want to use to evaluate your options. These criteria could relate to the potential consequences, stakeholders impacted by the decision, long-term benefits, or the resources or effort required. Give each criteria a weight or number of points to use when you're rating your options. Draw a table and list the criteria along one side of the table and your list of alternatives on the other side of the table to form an "L". Lastly, measure each criterion against each choice you have and record the rating. A decision matrix is useful when you need to compare multiple options against a set of weighted criteria. It's an objective and structured way to make a decision.

Criterion	Weight	House A		House B		House C	
		Score	Weighted	Score	Weighted	Score	Weighted
Purchase Price	0.25	4	1.00	3	0.75	5	1.25
Location	0.20	5	1.00	4	0.80	3	0.60
Size/Layout	0.15	3	0.45	5	0.75	4	0.60
Commute Time	0.10	2	0.20	4	0.40	3	0.30
School Quality	0.10	4	0.40	3	0.30	5	0.50
Maintenance	0.10	2	0.20	4	0.40	2	0.20
Resale Value	0.10	5	0.50	3	0.30	4	0.40
	Total	3.75		3.70		3.85	
	Rank	2		3		1	

Figure 5: Decision Matrix

A SWOT analysis (Figure 6) helps you analyze the strengths, weaknesses, opportunities, and threats relating to your decision and its solutions. List these four factors in a grid to create a helpful visual comparison of your options. Strengths of your options are the positive consequences of that option, the ways it solves the problem, and its long-term benefits in solving the problem. Weaknesses of your alternatives are what could be improved about the solution, what should be avoided when applying this solution, and how it could be counter-productive to solving the problem. Opportunities are features of the solution that allow for potentially positive outcomes of implementing the solution that may not be apparent at first glance. When listing opportunities for your solutions, remain realistic instead of being idealistic. Opportunities can also be features of the solution that help you make future decisions. Threats are external factors that can negatively impact how your solution will work once it's implemented. Threats are usually not within your control but shouldn't be overlooked because life doesn't happen in a vacuum. Identifying threats early on can help you choose a solution that is iron-clad for that particular problem. Use SWOT analysis to navigate difficult decisions where the stakes are high.

Figure 6: SWOT Analysis

Exercise 21: Tool Test Drive

Learning which tool to use for the variety of decisions you'll need to make in your career and personal life can set you up for success as a critical thinker. This takes practice and developing a routine of trying each tool until you're comfortable with applying these tools to your decision-making process. This exercise will help you pair the best tool with the appropriate decision.

1. Write down a major decision you need to make within the next six months. It could be financial, career-based, or a personal one.

2. Draw a decision tree with your decision at the root and your options as nodes joined by branches to each other and their consequences.

3. Create a simple decision matrix where you list three or four possible solutions and rate them against the same number of criteria, which are weighted. The criteria could include cost, impact, and effort.

4. Map out a SWOT analysis of at least one of your potential options.

5. Reflect on your application of each tool to your decision and particularly pay attention to whether these tools helped you see something new about the decision or clarify your thinking pattern.

Gut vs. Logic—When to Trust Which

You've probably heard the phrase "trust your gut" when you're faced with a tough decision, and we tend to place trusting our gut instincts and using reason and logic on opposite ends of the decision-making spectrum. However, when using critical thinking, you'll find that logic and your gut instincts are equally important to building your decision-making muscle. Your gut instincts are based on your intuition or feelings about a situation without exploring any data, evidence, or logical reasoning. You might even struggle to justify your gut feelings, but you just know they're right. Examples of when you might use your gut instincts are when you're deciding whether or not to trust someone you've just met, or when you feel you need to visit a family member or friend you haven't seen in a long time. These are fairly simple decisions; however, when it comes to more complicated decisions like making a major career change or buying that house you've been dreaming of, you might be reluctant to trust your gut instead of using data, statistics, and logical reasoning to make the decision.

Making decisions based on your gut instinct results are quick decisions based on a combination of your emotional state at the time and your life experience. These decisions are made unconsciously and without a second thought. Our emotions and experiences are powerful driving forces that influence our choices, but relying solely on them to navigate life and scrutinize complex issues can mislead us into making the wrong choice. Relying on your gut instincts works best when you're an expert or are deeply familiar with a situation. Using logic to make decisions involves a slower process of gathering evidence and analyzing it within the structured framework of reason. Logical reasoning is a conscious process and is better for making complex decisions because it creates objectivity while removing emotion. The sweet spot for making decisions that solve a problem holistically is to combine and balance both your intuition and logical reasoning. This combination is used by trained professionals who have to make quick and important decisions regularly. Think of first responders arriving at a fire or car pile-up, doctors working in emergency care, detectives who have to assess suspects, and lawyers who have to decide how to pivot while in the courtroom. These professionals combine their training and their instincts to function in stressful situations every day. When you need to make a complex decision, it's essential to use your intuition to alert your logical reasoning to kick in and then to use that logic to verify your gut instinct.

Exercise 22: The Gut Check Reflection

When making a decision, it can be a game-changer to write everything down to give you a helpful visual to guide both your logic and gut instincts. The objective of this exercise is to flip the switch on solely relying on data and logic or on your unverified intuition and hopefully nurture your thinking that a combination of the two works best with most decisions.

1. Recall a recent decision where you went with your gut instinct and another where you only relied on logic to make your decision.

2. Reflect on each decision by writing down the following for each:

   a. Your goal for each decision.

   b. All of your possible solutions, decisions, or options.

   c. The pros and cons of each decision.

   d. The worst-case scenario you had in mind if you made the wrong decision.

   e. Who else would the decision impact besides you.

3. Write down your reflections on whether you would make the same decisions again, and if there was a way to combine both your instincts and logic.

Key Takeaways

You'll learn how to reach out to others and collaborate using critical thinking to solve problems as a team in the next chapter, but let's review the skills you've learned to make confident and informed decisions:

- The basic decision-making process involves seven steps: defining your decision, collecting evidence, investigating alternative solutions, evaluating your options, deciding on a solution, implementing your solution, and reviewing the impact of your solution.

- The tools you can use to make decisions are the decision tree, which helps you map out consequences, the decision matrix, which makes objective decisions, and the SWOT analysis for complex decisions.

- Your gut instincts and logical reasoning must work together when making decisions because they combine the critical thinking process and your life experience.

Chapter Eight

People Smart

Thinking Better Together

It is the mark of an educated mind to be able to entertain a thought without accepting it.

Aristotle

Your journey to improve your critical thinking has so far been focused on your individual thinking routine and using critical thinking to make decisions that impact you. However, in reality, you have to use critical thinking while collaborating with others to reach a solution. It's impossible to gain knowledge and different opinions without branching out from your internal thoughts about critical thinking and listening to diverse opinions and facts. Think back to the analogy of hearing your favorite band play your favorite song. That's not the result of one individual, the music comes to life when all members of the band collaborate in harmony, knowing when to exercise restraint and when to showcase their skills on the song. Problem solving in a group works in a similar way. In this chapter, you'll lay the foundations to help you develop critical thinking skills in social settings, so that you can listen actively, engage in more productive conversations, and resist unhelpful group influence while you confidently contribute to making informed collective decisions.

How to Think Critically During Conversations

If you've been in a heated debate before with a friend or colleague with a different opinion from you, you both probably tried to outsmart each other by arguing each point with your own evidence until either one conceded or agreed to disagree on the topic. These healthy debates are vital to socializing and keeping us intellectually engaged with our peers. Such conversations can be frustrating if you feel like you're not being heard by the other person or if you're not listening to what they're saying and just listening until you find a point to jump in with an even better story. Entering a formal or informal discussion with the desire to "win" at all costs prevents you from locking your critical thinking skills into gear to make the most out of the conversation. For example, you and a colleague might discuss the best way to motivate your team. You believe a team social or team-building exercise out of the office would work best, while your colleague believes that monetary incentives are the only way to go. The discussion gets heated and ends with your colleague storming off and accusing you of not wanting your team to be financially successful. Critical thinking was kicked to the curb in favor of emotion, logical fallacies, and biases.

Thinking critically during any conversation, no matter how complex, should start with respecting the person you're conversing with. They're a person with history, context, and their own story, just like you. You can show this by leaning in as they're speaking, affirming that they've raised good points, and nodding your head to show you're listening. You need to leave your mind open to the possibility of being proved wrong and open to new solutions you never considered before the conversation. Curiosity is a pillar of critical thinking, and truly listening to the other person allows you to remain curious about their perspective. Ask them questions to clarify their points and get a good idea of their angle on the problem. Separating the facts from your own and the other person's opinions is essential to thinking critically during conversations. Opinions can trigger emotional responses and leave the discussion without any resolution, so avoid leaning into assumptions and call them out if you have to. Keep the goal, decision, or solution you're both trying to reach in mind to avoid getting distracted by red herrings and having your emotional buttons pushed. Solutions are more likely if you find common ground than if you each try to win the argument.

Exercise 23: The 5-Minute Replay

Conversations where critical thinking has left the room can lead to conflict, frustration, and a stalemate between the parties. Not every conversation is comfortable or casual, but you can trust in applying critical thinking to get you through even the difficult conversations. The objective of this exercise is to elevate your awareness of how you can apply the critical thinking skills you've learned to everyday conversations at work, home, or socially.

1. After your next memorable conversation, be it casual or formal, write down the following:

    a. A fact that you heard.

    b. An opinion that you heard.

c. A question you could have asked the other parties.

d. How you conducted yourself during the conversation.

e. How would you've liked to conduct yourself differently using a critical thinking lens?

2. Repeat this exercise with three different types of conversations (personal, work-related, and casual) you have had during this week.

Listening for Understanding, Not for Defending

There's a difference between listening to understand and listening to reply or to defend your point. You might've found yourself zoning out during a conversation and not listening to the other person, or you might be so offended by their point of view that you're like a boxer waiting to be allowed into the ring to counter every point made with your own. Active listening is an important part of the critical thinking process and requires you to abandon the notion of "winning" during a conversation and the practice of just passively hearing what's being said. You need to shift your mindset from waiting to talk or wanting to hear to wanting to understand. By opening your mind to the other person in the conversation and working with them to interpret what they're saying, you can validly dispute their points with a properly constructed argument, evidence, and reach a productive middle ground or solution.

Active listening requires a combination of genuine curiosity, positive body language towards the person you're listening to, and abandoning your assumptions and desire to "win" by turning the discussion into a conflict. You can actively engage with the other person by pausing the conversation after they've made a point to reflect on it, paraphrase what they've said, and relate it back to them along the lines of "So to summarize your point..." or "So what you're saying is...". Asking questions about their points, evidence, or how they reached their conclusions is a great way to move the conversation forward and keep it productive. Observing the other person's body language can give you cues as to how to interpret what they're saying. Take note of their tone when speaking, the pacing of their words, and whether their body language is defensive or open. These cues can help you calibrate how you converse with them and give you a deeper understanding of their words. Avoid falling into the trap of over-confidence, arrogance, or triggering the other person's emotions when you're actively listening. Listening to them to get a "gotcha" moment where you're able to catch them out on an incorrect or contradictory point will make you focus on your counterpart's flaws instead of looking for the deeper meaning of their words and how you can reach a solution. Active listening can especially help you in your work environment to gain insight into your customers or colleagues, and in your personal life because actively listening to your loved ones will help you deepen those important connections with them.

Exercise 24: Echo and Ask

Common examples of when active listening is ignored in favor of defending and passively hearing are during arguments between spouses and between parents and children. These conversations can be difficult because emotions are involved, but critical thinking can make them go smoother and result in long-term resolution. Conversations about your performance at work with your leaders could be difficult to listen to, if the feedback isn't all positive, but this exercise will help you gain the necessary insight from such conversations to improve yourself and how you interpret information.

1. During at least one conversation you have today, take the following two steps to show you're actively listening:

    a. Paraphrase what the other person is saying before you reply or make your point.

    b. Ask a follow-up question that shows that you're trying to understand their point of view, instead of debating with them and winning an argument.

2. Reflect on the results of these steps afterwards. Write down if the other person's behavior towards you was positive and collaborative, and if you felt that the steps you took to actively listen added depth to your interaction with them.

Handling Groupthink and Peer Pressure

The need to belong to a group or collective is a basic human need that we've all felt at some point. Whether you followed the latest trends in fashion and music at school to keep up with your peers, or you're reluctant to disagree with a popular co-worker at the office, you've experienced the need to conform and not upset the status quo of a group. The action of agreeing or going along with the majority to stay part of the group can lead to the concept known as groupthink. Groupthink happens when a group puts its cohesion and unity above logic and reason. Favoring the group's opinion to maintain the status quo leads to the group making irrational decisions without using critical thinking. Peer pressure occurs when the group tries to influence an individual into agreeing with the group opinion instead of thinking for themselves. This pressure to conform can lead to groupthink prevailing in a group where there may be people with different opinions.

Despite popular culture, peer pressure can be positive if it leads to the individual being influenced to have positive values. For example, your friend group could peer pressure you into joining the gym, which is good for your health. However, if they suddenly start telling you not to be friends with people who don't also go to the gym because they aren't friends with such people, then groupthink has crept in and led to an attempt to influence you into irrational and negative decisions. Giving into groupthink counteracts your critical thinking skills because it causes you to censor your opinions and beliefs when they don't align with the group. Groupthink can also make you lean into your confirmation bias because if the group's opinions align with your own, you'll be more likely to agree with their decisions. There's a false sense of anonymity that goes along with decisions made by groupthink because the group acts as one in its decision, even if it's irrational. Examples of the negative impact of groupthink can be seen in cases where a mob mentality and vigilante justice have harmed innocent people. Comments sections on social media platforms where people engage in cyberbullying others, just because everyone else is doing it is another common example.

Combating groupthink and peer pressure in a work or social environment can be challenging, but it's not impossible because of the benefits of critical thinking. Critical thinking is the arch-nemesis of groupthink and its negative impacts. Thinking for yourself and rationalizing your own opinions and beliefs is crucial to avoid falling victim to groupthink as an individual. If you're leading a group or team socially or at work and you need to solve a problem, you can prevent groupthink from creeping in, even if you all share common opinions or beliefs. Your starting point should be collaboration instead of conflict or compromise. Try to recognize the signs of groupthink and call them out before they take hold. These signs include members of the group agreeing with an opinion without questioning it, remaining silent instead of voicing their concerns, and other members pressuring them to conform to the group's views. Encouraging the group to be open-minded and curious by investigating opposing perspectives is another way to prevent groupthink. Your group should use data and logic as anchors to keep the discussion grounded in reality and free from biases or emotional responses. By centralizing logic and data, you can ask important questions to challenge assumptions like "What are we missing?" or "What if we're wrong and there's another way to solve this?". Bear in mind that you're here to change the group's ideas and not change the character of the people within the group.

Exercise 25: Devil's Advocate Drill

Playing devil's advocate means challenging an accepted opinion or premise to encourage a debate and explore a different perspective on an argument. The objective of this exercise is to keep your critical thinking skills sharp when you're leading or part of a group situation to avoid caving to peer pressure or allowing groupthink to manifest in the group.

1. Choose an upcoming or hypothetical group discussion that you'd have at work, at home, or socially to deconstruct.

2. Identify the dominant viewpoint or opinion on the topic of discussion.

3. Write down two or three alternative explanations, perspectives, risks, or ideas that haven't been considered by the group.

4. Role-play or practice how you would raise one of the alternative points while discussing the topic with the group. Always be respectful to those you're discussing with.

5. Apply these steps to a discussion in a real group setting and write down your reflections on your actions to present a different angle and the group's reaction to this.

Key Takeaways

The next chapter continues to expand your critical thinking survival kit by exploring how to keep your cool and think critically when you're in stressful situations. Let's recap what you've learned about critical thinking in a group so you can combine it with the skills coming up in the next chapter:

- Thinking critically during conversations with others requires listening to understand instead of listening to reply, maintaining respect for the other person, wanting to achieve a mutual understanding of the problem instead of winning an argument, and separating facts from opinions.

- Active listening is an important critical thinking skill and can be achieved by observing the other person's body language, affirming and summarizing the points they've raised, abandoning the need to defend your points by catching the other person out, and asking clarifying questions.

- Preventing a mob mentality or groupthink from festering in a group setting, you need to recognize and call out the signs of groupthink, ask questions to challenge assumptions, and rely on data and logic to verify points and reasons for opinions.

Chapter Nine

Thinking Under Pressure

Staying Sharp When It Counts

I refuse to answer that question on the grounds that I don't know the answer.

Douglas Adams

S tress isn't an aspect of your life that should be minimized. Your stress could stem from a rushed morning routine, an intense day of meeting ahead of you at work, a family issue that's been difficult to resolve, or your finances. Stress can crop up daily, even hourly, and impact you in various physical, emotional, and mental ways. Much of the stress we experience is due to decision fatigue because we have to constantly make decisions from the moment we wake up until we turn in for the day. Applying the critical thinking process can make both simpler and complex decisions easier for you, where you rely on your practiced thinking routine to make certain decisions. However, when the pressure is suddenly turned up a notch in a crisis or a high stakes situation where stress starts to battle with your rational mind for dominance, it becomes difficult to think critically and calmly. In this chapter, we'll explore solutions to prevent stress from winning this battle. You'll develop the ability to stay mentally sharp, focused, and rational when you're under pressure. You'll learn how to manage your stress effectively by applying simple and practical tools to your real life.

Managing Stress and Mental Overload

Statistics indicate that 37% of people are more likely to operate with lower cognitive function when their stress levels are elevated (Schimelpfening, 2023). This shows that your stress levels have a direct impact on your mental well-being, and stress can impact your ability to learn, absorb, and process information, your memory, and your concentration levels (Schimelpfening, 2023). Feelings of stress can be triggered when you're feeling overwhelmed, under pressure, and when you're faced with tasks that seem impossible to complete. Stress is deceptive in that you feel it coming on in bursts for short periods of time, and then it seems to disappear once you've overcome the decision, task, or situation that initially brought it on. However, the impacts of stress, even for the short-term, can negatively impact your body and mind. Stress manifests as feeling sad, avoiding activities you used to enjoy, feeling anxious, feeling irritated, stomach cramps, digestion issues, neck pain, headaches, feeling hopeless, overeating, not eating enough, insomnia, oversleeping, a lack of clarity in your thinking, the inability to focus, and seeing every situation through a negative or an "impossibility" lens.

Learning to manage stress is important because your life will never be completely stress-free, and trying to achieve an unrealistic stress-free life can exacerbate your stress levels and symptoms, causing permanent damage. Stress affects how you make decisions because people tend to revert to emotional reactions and their brains' shortcuts or biases when they feel overwhelmed, either by the decision, the stakes, or the information behind it. Grab hold of your life right now and start managing your stress from the inside out. This means starting to manage the impact stress is having on your mental abilities, which usually helps the physical impacts find their way to the exit. Consciously bringing about your sense of mental calmness doesn't mean you're ignoring your stress; it means you're actively trying to help your mind and body bounce back from its negative impact.

The first step to managing stress is to avoid a mental overload by freeing up your mental real estate for deep, proactive thinking instead of fast, reactive, and emotional thinking. Apply the mental decluttering techniques that you've explored in previous chapters. Next, understand that self-care practices boost your brain's cognitive abilities. The current "hustle culture" where social media influencers encourage you to be constantly working on multiple things, is missing the point of critical thinking. You need to be calm and allow your mind to focus. Getting enough sleep, staying hydrated, eating enough nutrients, getting your body moving, and taking breaks during work periods are not luxuries. These are tools required to stimulate your critical thinking abilities. Learning how to recognize and manage your stress will help you think clearly, rationally, and objectively. It will also make your critical thinking muscles more adaptable, resilient, and resistant to emotional thinking and mental shortcuts when you're under pressure.

Exercise 26: Stress Audit

Recognizing what triggers your stress and taking small steps to work on your stress symptoms can help you free up that prime mental real estate to remove unhelpful negative and unrealistic thoughts and replace them with critical thinking skills. This exercise is meant to help you recognize what brings on your stress responses, what those responses are, and get creative in eliminating those responses.

1. Write down three recent situations where your stress levels made it difficult for you to think clearly. These could be related to work or your personal life.

2. Note the signs and symptoms you noticed physically in or on your body, on your mental state, and on your general thoughts.

3. Write down at least two solutions you could implement the next time to reduce your mental overload when these stressful situations occur again. Examples include turning off your notifications on your phone, taking a break from work, or deep breathing.

How to Think Clearly in a Crisis

When you're stressed, your cognitive bandwidth is restricted because your brain has shifted focus from intentional analysis, deep-thinking, being open-minded, and creativity to survival mode and fast reactions. This is because stressful situations place your body and mind in a state of fight-or-flight mode. Your brain reverts to the quickest, easiest, automatic, and most comforting shortcuts or biases and this affects the clarity of the decisions you make when you're stressed. Your decisions should be made from a point of calmness and not from a place of emotion and stress. This is easier said than done because life is far from linear, and a financial, career, personal, or even political crisis could hit at any time and pull you into a state of stress. However, any crisis can be dealt with by taking a moment to pause, slow down, and attempt to structure your thoughts. When you're stressed, you might see slowing down as a waste of time, but you'll achieve far more and come up with useful solutions if you take a beat to calm down instead of trying to act in a panic.

Structuring your thoughts and emotions in a crisis means acknowledging them but not engaging with them or locking them in while you find the best way forward. Separating yourself from your stress reactions can bring about mental clarity and help you ground yourself in the reality of the crisis by stepping outside of your usual stress cycle without panicking (Abedinpour, 2024). Next, untangle what you can't control from what you can. This will help you zero in on useful actions instead of feeling overwhelmed and not achieving anything to stop the crisis. Your emotions need to be acknowledged but not engaged with for the moment because they're hardly ever useful in a crisis, and they can distort your perspective of reality, especially during a stressful time. Next, you can use the entire or part of the decision-making process previously discussed to come up with a solution quickly. Lastly, once the dust has settled, reframe the crisis as a learning experience or a step on a path to something bigger for you. Ask yourself how you can learn, grow, and find opportunities from the crisis, and how you dealt with it. Reframing can shift your perspective from a negative to a positive.

Thinking clearly in a crisis can be done by having a plan in mind in case the crisis does in fact happen. Don't confuse mental preparation with overthinking or catastrophizing something that hasn't even happened.

Preparation in terms of critical thinking means being adaptable, embracing uncertainty, and building up your brain's resilience to think clearly in tough times. You can do this by developing a network of people who you know will be there to support you and help keep you calm during a crisis, developing a step-by-step plan if the crisis is something you know is going to happen in the near future, and focusing solely on what you can control in every situation and managing stress that comes with the aspects you can't control.

Exercise 27: Crisis Clarity Drill

You can practice thinking clearly during stressful situations by taking the following steps: acknowledging your emotions and mental shortcuts, separating your emotions from the facts, prioritizing the decisions you need to make in the crisis and by when you need to make them, reframing the crisis as growth or an opportunity, working on keeping your critical thinking skills agile and resilient in preparation for the next crisis, and being kind to yourself by allowing for time to recover from dealing with the crisis. This exercise will allow you to implement these steps in stressful situations you might encounter.

1. Consider a situation that might cause you to panic. Examples include missing a flight, having to rush a loved one to the hospital, having to receive or give bad news, or preparing for an important deliverable at work.

2. List three questions you can ask yourself in the moment the crisis manifests as a reality. Examples include "What is in my control here?", "What's the first thing I can do to help?", or "Do I know someone who can help with this situation?".

3. Write down a crisis plan of the steps you'd take and the decisions you'd need to make to solve the crisis you chose. Reflect on whether these steps required critical thinking and intentional decisions or were motivated by emotional reactions.

4. Write down a 10-point checklist of helpful self-talk affirmations you can refer to during a crisis.

Practicing to Pause, Breathe, and Think

Stress is like a fog that's triggered by your feelings of being overwhelmed, emotional, or anxious. Allowing that fog to get even murkier with over-thinking, negative self-talk, and focusing on the problem instead of the solution will take you further away from clear thinking. Clearing that fog requires you to clear your mind. This means more than ignoring your stress and your emotions or letting them go into the ether. Truly clearing your mind means acknowledging your stress, making mental clarity your goal, and deliberately pursuing it through the techniques that work for you. Mental clarity is achieved through being mindful, which means being aware of and observing your thoughts, processing them, and learning how to replace your panicked thinking with your critical thinking routine.

The first step to clearing the fog of stress is to deliberately pause what you're doing. Pausing interrupts what you're doing and your reaction to the situation. Simply standing up, moving to a different room, or even to a different part of the room, and taking a moment to stop makes a difference. Even just one second of stillness can transform a reaction into a decision. An example of the power of the pause can be seen in competitive reality cooking shows, where contestants are put under immense pressure in terms of time and quality. They're panicking and frantic until they step outside of the studio (often in a dramatic fashion) and take a moment to collect themselves before returning with a newfound sense of energy and determination.

Next, simply breathe. Breathing exercises, not necessarily full-on meditation, can help you calm your nervous system from the jitters caused by stress and become fully present in the moment. Close your eyes and slip into the moment of your pause for at least 30 seconds the next time you're in a crisis. A slow and deep breath is your body's way of telling your brain that it's safe to think again. The last step to combating your reaction to stress is to think. Thinking clearly isn't possible if you don't take the time to pause and then breathe, so don't jump straight to this step because you'll end up repeating your stress cycle. Making thinking about the crisis your final step allows you to let your critical thinking muscles and the decision-making process kick in to solve the problem instead of just ruminating about the stress aspect of it.

The following personal example might further illuminate the benefits of the pause, think, breathe routine. My flying instructor taught me that when a problem occurs for a pilot, you always have limited time to assess the situation before making a decision. It's important to think about the problem before reacting because your immediate reaction might be incorrect. Another lesson he stressed is to always fly the plane. Lives have been lost because the pilot was dealing with a situation instead of flying the plane. When I'm stressed or in a crisis, I tell myself to "always fly the plane". This reminds me to pause, consider what's happening, and make a decision instead of mentally shutting down, which could cause a much bigger problem.

Exercise 28: The 60-Second Reset

Mindfulness, and your pause, breathe, and think routine, doesn't have to take 30 minutes, where you might add to your stress by forcing yourself to schedule this exercise. This exercise is meant to be applied in a crisis, on the fly, when you have "no time to think". So, be kind to yourself and remember that stress is normal and inevitable in life.

1. Set a timer for 60 seconds and think of a situation that's been making you feel stressed.

2. Pause by placing both of your feet on the ground, relaxing your shoulders, and unclenching your jaw.

3. Breathe by taking three deep and slow breaths in and out, each lasting at least three seconds. Count to three if you have to.

4. Think by asking "What matters the most right now?" or "What can I do right now to help the situation?"

5. Use this routine daily during your moments or low stress to build up the habit mentally and physically.

Key Takeaways

The next and final chapter will guide you on how to lock down your critical thinking routine for the long-term and become an intentional thinker for the rest of your life with small but effective habits. Let's review what you've learned about stress, managing it, and how to prevent it from influencing your thinking and decisions:

- Stress can impact your cognitive abilities, mental health, and physical health. Stress is inevitable and must be managed through recognition of your stress triggers, mental decluttering, and self-care routines.

- You can think clearly in a crisis by acknowledging your stress and emotions but not engaging with them, untangling the facts from your feelings, reframing the crisis as a learning opportunity, embracing uncertainty, and ensuring your mind is adaptable and resilient to sudden change through critical thinking practices.

- Stressful situations can be managed by developing the pause, breathe, and think routine to give yourself the best chance of not becoming overwhelmed by stress and using your critical thinking skills in a crisis.

Chapter Ten

Daily Practice, Lifelong Skill

Cementing Your Thinking Habits

I have not failed. I've just found 10,000 ways that won't work.

Thomas Edison

So often, we're shamed into believing that a lack of willpower and our inherently flawed human nature are the reasons why we fail to stick to good habits. This negative self-talk crops up if you've slipped up on your gym routine, healthy diet, or regular meetups with friends. However, relating habits solely to willpower, discipline, and blaming ourselves for not sticking to them is incorrect. For habits to stick, they need to be unpacked, built into a convenient and accessible system or routine. Keeping your critical thinking skills sharp is no different from sticking to a positive eating or exercise habit. In this chapter, you'll explore how to turn your critical thinking skills into lasting mental habits through intentional and daily routines, reflection practices, and strategies. Your focus should be on your long-term intellectual growth and cognition that goes beyond the 31-day plan you've been following so far.

Designing a Critical Thinking Routine

Your thinking routine, just like your exercise routine, should be consistent in how often you practice it instead of intense over short bursts of times. A short and daily thinking routine is better than doing an occasional deep dive with your thinking when you're in an emergency. To keep your thinking routine consistent, you'll need to make it a habit. Forming a habit means understanding that habits are made up of three components that form a loop: cues, routines, and rewards. In terms of critical thinking, a cue could be you reading or watching your news feed in the morning before work or school, and you pick up on a story that sparks your interest. The routine involves the steps or actions you take after receiving the cue. Your routine could be that you go to social media to research the story, where your feed is full of people who share the same opinions as you on the story. The reward is the gain you receive from following the cue and engaging your routine. The reward tells your brain that this habit loop is one you want to repeat in the future. Your reward would be seeing that your social media feed aligns with your views on the story, and you're satisfied that you've been proven right.

Grasping the habit loop concept means becoming self-aware and conscious that rewards are transient and shouldn't be the only reason you repeat habits. In the example above, the routine should be changed to explore other opinions on the story instead of just wanting to receive the reward of being proved correct. The reward should be that your critical thinking routine led you down a path of investigating the story holistically, and you fact-checked the evidence to draw a conclusion, even if it went against your opinion. Developing a new thinking routine that will stick starts by writing down your thinking habits, the biases you lean into, and what you'd like to change about these habits. This will give you a good foundation to build your new thinking routine. Next, work on anchoring your thinking routine to another routine you engage in daily, like drinking your morning coffee in your kitchen or brushing your teeth. Next, make sure your thinking routine is simple and sustainable. You can do this by starting with small, repeatable steps to prevent yourself from feeling overwhelmed about changing everything at once. Lastly, you should track your progress of thinking within your new thinking system by using a visual tracker like a journal or a vision board to assess your growth as a critical thinker.

A thinking routine you can try out every day is an observational everyday called "See, Think, Wonder" (Bown, 2021). This routine encourages observation, interpretation, assessing evidence, and asking questions, which are all essential to critical thinking. Try this by observing something during your day. This could be an interaction between co-workers, an advertisement you see along your commute, or a post on your social media. feed. Ask yourself what you see, what you think is going on, and what you're wondering about what you see (Bown, 2021). This routine can immediately challenge your biases and assumptions, and it engages your sense of curiosity. Another critical thinking routine you can apply is called "Headlines," where you focus on big picture thinking and the essence of a situation. Choose something to observe during your day and ask yourself what headline you'd choose to write to capture the most important parts of what you've observed. This routine is a good one to use within a group because everyone might see the headline of an issue differently, and this helps you explore different perspectives.

Exercise 29: Create Your 5-Minute Thinking Routine

As stressful as life can be, it's well worth your time to develop a structured critical thinking routine that you can easily follow each day. It will keep your brain alert and hone your critical thinking skills. This exercise helps you customize your critical thinking routine for your lifestyle into a workable system.

1. Create a list of 10 questions or prompts you want to ask yourself to reflect on your critical thinking routine for that day. Include questions such as "What assumptions did I make today?", "What decisions did I make today and how did I deal with them?", or "Did any of my biases emerge in my thinking today?"

2. Choose a time during the day when you have at least five minutes of silence to think. It could be the morning, during your lunch break, or in the evenings.

3. Choose one prompt from your list and write down and reflect on your answers.

4. Commit to answering the same question for the next seven days to observe your thinking habits and how to change them.

5. Use a habit tracker app or your calendar to check off each day you practice this routine and reward yourself for completing the exercise.

Journaling and Reflection Techniques

Developing your sense of self-awareness has been a recurring theme throughout your 31-day critical thinking journey. From a practical perspective, self-awareness with critical thinking requires you to engage in metacognition, which is the practice of thinking about thinking. This practice allows you to reflect on your thinking habits and how you process information that you observe. Reflection is a powerful concept because thinking on autopilot without looking internally leaves room for biases and assumptions to creep in. However, through reflection, you can get a firm grip on how you think, what thinking routines work for you, and how you can improve your thinking within the critical thinking framework. Gaining insight into yourself and how you think makes you a better communicator with those around you because you'll be confident and aware enough to challenge assumptions, draw conclusions using logic, and explore different angles of a problem without being afraid of being proved wrong.

Cementing these concepts and making metacognition part of your life as a critical thinker requires a method to keep track of your progress. Journaling is a great way to do this because writing something down helps you identify recurring thoughts, biases, and blind spots to reveal thinking patterns and leverage points to upgrade them. Journaling prompts can become powerful tools that help you reflect on the aspects of critical thinking you need to focus on to improve. When journaling, focus on prompts that stimulate metacognition. This will allow you to revisit your thinking, and looking back at your journal entries per week or per month can help you recognize insights you didn't notice at the moment your first wrote them down. It will help you monitor your progress and areas for improvement. Consider your journal as your thinking bank and your reflections or insights as extra income that you can invest in the areas you need to work on.

Exercise 30: Critical Reflection Journal

Throughout this 31-day journey, you've hopefully kept a journal to track your answers to each exercise. This can become your critical thinking journal where you record your reflections, improvement plans, and progress. This exercise is intended to make your critical thinking journal part of your daily thinking routine.

1. Choose three journal prompts to rotate during the next week. These could include the following:

    a. What went well today in the way I thought something through?

    b. How did my thinking fail me today?

    c. When did my thinking feel rushed?

    d. What did I change my mind about today?

    e. What biases cropped up in my thinking today?

2. Write down a few sentences or paragraphs for each prompt you chose.

3. After seven days, review your entries for that week and highlight any recurring themes or opportunities for growth.

Keeping the Momentum After 31 Days

There's an established structural framework that applies to critical thinking, i.e., identifying the problem, gathering evidence, analyzing the evidence, considering alternative viewpoints, drawing logical conclusions based on the evidence, and implementing the solutions. However, critical thinking isn't a stagnant or uniform concept because it stimulates your brain to think in an agile, adaptable, and emotionally resilient way. Your critical thinking skills will definitely evolve over time if you consistently apply your thinking routines and strive to become more self-aware. The 31-day plan you've worked so hard on to kick start your critical thinking journey is just a springboard to facilitate your leaps onto the complex problems and topics you'll be faced with in your daily life.

The current age of technology and the information overload require you to remain agile and resilient in your thinking. It's becoming more difficult to find the objective truth with social media and every possible opinion gaining traction through each platform. Keep yourself in check by scheduling monthly check-ins with your critical thinking skills because periodic reviews keep your progress aligned with your long-term goals. Variety in thought is essential to keeping your skills razor sharp, so work on building up an intellectually supportive network of friends or colleagues. Finding a community to engage with others who also value thoughtful discussion and different perspectives will incorporate critical thinking into your lifestyle. Turn the spark of critical thought that you've lit up over these 31 days into a raging fire by continuously learning through intellectually valuable books, podcasts, or courses. Stimulating your intellect is an investment in yourself because it can refresh and deepen your critical thinking skills.

Exercise 31: Design Your Long-Term Thinking Growth Plan

Keeping yourself engaged with the way you think and how to improve it is a priceless skill that will keep your brain sharp well into your later years. This final exercise is intended to make critical thinking, healthy debate, and self-awareness part of your journey through life.

1. Answer the following questions:

   a. What aspect of my thinking do I want to keep improving?

   b. What's one monthly challenge or goal I can set? For example, challenge one assumption a day.

   c. Who or what can help me stay accountable? For example, find a thinking partner, do a monthly journaling review, or join a podcast club.

2. Write down your critical thinking plan for the next three months, with one activity or goal planned for each month.

Key Takeaways

Before we conclude the start of your lifelong critical thinking journey, let's recap the tools you now have in your kit to cement your critical thinking skills.

- Habits are made up of cues, routines, and rewards and will only stick if they are simple, convenient, and consistently practiced.

- Starting a critical thinking journal can help you identify thinking patterns, biases, and opportunities to improve your thinking routines.

- Critical thinking isn't a stagnant concept, and training yourself to consistently apply it requires investing your time and effort into your critical thinking growth plan.

Conclusion

You've Got This! Keep Growing and Stay Sharp

If your actions create a legacy that inspires others to dream more, learn more, do more, and become more, then you are an excellent leader.

Dolly Parton

Each step you've taken on this path to expand your knowledge about critical thinking has contributed to your intellectual growth. You've learned more about yourself, the way you think, and how to build on the already solid foundation that exists. Critical thinking and your grip on it isn't a stagnant concept, it's a structural framework that you can adapt and apply in your daily life to make informed decisions that help to light your path in life. As we reflect on your 31-day critical thinking journey, it's important that you embrace a mindset of continuous improvement without being held back by self-criticism and the pursuit of perfection.

Celebrate Progress, Not Perfection

Self-improvement requires consistency, brutal honesty, reflection, and resilience. The steps you've already taken to improve your critical thinking count as important progress in your growth. You've learned how to keep your critical thinking skills sharp by managing the impact that stress has on your ability to make decisions when under pressure. You learned how to cement the critical thinking habits you've picked up by understanding and applying the concept of the habit loop of cues, routines, and rewards, journaling, and reflection to your critical thinking routine to learn more about how you think. The techniques you've explored allow you to celebrate the smaller critical thinking every day wins to build your momentum and confidence as an analytical thinker. Taking the time to reflect on your personal growth adds fuel to the fire of motivation within you and increases your brain's resilience to adapt your critical thinking skills to various environments. By applying concepts like the pause, breathe, and think routine and scheduling check-ins with yourself about your thinking, you'll understand that mistakes or flawed thinking are valuable data, and not failures. Accept the reality that achieving perfection in your thinking is a myth and that the true sign of mastery in motion is consistent progress.

Thinking Like a Lifelong Learner

In building your 31-day critical thinking foundation, you've learned that critical thinking is a practice to master, not a destination or a state of being to reach. We started your journey by decluttering your mind to create room for curiosity, which keeps your thinking flexible, creative, and sharp. You revealed the shortcuts your brain might be relying on to make quick decisions through your cognitive biases. However, our exploration of the power of questions and how to ask the right ones challenged your biases and proved that exposure to different perspectives can expand your cognitive toolkit. Evaluating evidence is another powerful tool you now have access to, where you can analyze the source and context of a piece of data to determine its value. The concept of logic, logical fallacies, and how to spot them are lifelong skills that will help you maintain your emotional maturity and sense of calm in any future argument. You also explored the structure of arguments, i.e., a conclusion drawn from a premise using evidence, and we covered the different types of reasoning you can use to build the bridge to connect your premise to your conclusion. You've eliminated the fear of being wrong about something because mastering the skill of drawing rational and logical conclusions based on evidence is more valuable than winning an argument.

Delving into the concept of systems thinking sets you up to see critical thinking as a structural framework that you can apply in different situations. Understanding that a problem exists within a system containing interconnected components, which are all connected to a bigger system within the world, is a powerful tool to help you deconstruct complex problems into their components that can be fixed. Mastering the steps of the critical thinking process by identifying the problem, gathering evidence about it, evaluating this evidence, and drawing conclusions or solutions based on logic will help you develop a constant loop of learning throughout your life.

Your Next Step—Real-Life Challenges to Tackle

In our exploration of the decision-making process and how to apply critical thinking skills to a group setting, you learned that critical thinking shines brightest as a cognitive tool when it's applied to everyday life situations. The 7-step decision-making process of defining your decision, collecting evidence, investigating alternative solutions, evaluating your options, deciding on a solution, implementing your solution, and reviewing the impact of your solution illustrates the positive results you can gain from the critical thinking process as a whole. The skills you learned will help you make informed and confident decisions.

Unpacking the concepts of groupthink, peer pressure, and active listening will help you make the most of opportunities to collaborate with others at work or socially to solve problems and discuss complex issues. Applying the critical thinking process helps you lead with logic instead of emotion, thereby avoiding the pitfalls of cognitive biases in your thinking and logical fallacies in your arguments. Listening to understand instead of listening to reply is an essential skill to master to elevate your critical thinking skills when you're having important meetings, discussing your relationships with your loved ones, or debating a topic that you're passionate about.

As you step out into the world and work towards success in your professional or academic career, or in your personal relationships, the lessons you've internalized through the exercises you've done over the last 31 days will make you a razor-sharp thinker. No matter what challenges or difficult decisions you face down the line, you'll have the self-awareness to see them as an opportunity to develop your critical thinking skills. This 31-day breakthrough you've worked so hard at means more than learning about abstract concepts. It's a meaningful step towards understanding your place in the world, how you think, how you make decisions, where your areas of improvement or biases lie, and how you want to frame your intellectual future. The last 31 days served as the flint to light the fire that illuminated your understanding of critical thinking. Help this flame burn brighter and stay alight by not shying away from life's problems that challenge your critical thinking skills and help you to stay motivated.

What is one question you should ask yourself every day that will improve your critical thinking? Sign up to the email list and you will receive this plus other tips to help your critical thinking skills. Use this link or QR code to find out! https://www .jaysissom.com/onequestion

About the Author

During my career as an IT and programming specialist, systems administrator, and teacher, I've learned that developing and increasing the mental tools we use to solve problems drastically improves life and our perspective on it. Throughout my career, I've been confronted with complex and sometimes overwhelming problems, and as I became more senior, the buck stopped at me to solve them. I realized that critical thinking and its components are a lifeline to any professional, entrepreneur, or student who is striving to operate at their mental best in their career and personal lives. Even now at 59, I use the critical thinking methods—that I'll be sharing with you—to navigate my career and my life with my family in Bloomington, Indiana, USA.

Learning has always been my passion, right from my humble beginnings in Indiana up to present day, where my hobbies encompass the more joyful parts of problem solving because I enjoy building electronic items from scratch, 3D printing and design, playing the piano, flying private aircraft, and reading science fiction novels about time travel. I believe that adopting a learning mindset will remove the teeth from any problem, no matter how monstrous or overwhelming it may seem in the moment. I decided to share the skills I've learned to broaden and sharpen my thinking habits to ensure that others are able to switch on the light of critical thinking to illuminate the darkness that's left by ignorance, succumbing to our biases and bad thinking habits, and turning our opinions into facts because they keep us mentally comfortable. Stepping out of your comfort zone leads to growth, and applying these lifelong critical thinking techniques is undoubtedly going to help you grow and thrive.

References

A, P. (2021, February 1). *Building a culture of critical thinking.* Linkedin. https://www.linkedin.com/pulse/building-culture-critical-thinking-prasad-a-s/

Abedinpour, P. (2024, September 16). *The Art of Thinking Clearly and Effectively in Tough Times.* Medium. https://medium.com/@peymaan.abedinpour/the-art-of-thinking-clearly-and-effectively-in-tough-times-3fedd1589049

Angélica Salomão. (2024, April 18). *Logical Precision: Crafting Strong Arguments.* Mind the Graph. https://mindthegraph.com/blog/sound-arguments/

Ashworth-Keppel, T. (2025, March 17). *How to improve your critical thinking skills.* Australian Institute of Business. https://www.aib.edu.au/blog/career-development/how-you-can-improve-your-critical-thinking-skills/

Bown, C. (2021, May 26). *6 Essential Thinking Routines you Need in your Repertoire.* Thinking Museum. https://thinkingmuseum.com/2021/05/26/6-essential-thinking-routines-you-need-in-your-repertoire/

Bracy, A. (2020, September 9). *Belief Systems And Self Awareness.* Trail Runner Magazine. https://www.trailrunnermag.com/training/mental-training-training/belief-systems-and-self-awareness/

Brietta, A. (2022, March 7). *Metacognition: The Science of Thinking About Thinking.* Riosalado College. https://www.riosalado.edu/news/2022/metacognition-science-thinking-about-thinking

Changing Habits. (n.d.). The Learning Center. Retrieved May 20, 2025, from https://learningcenter.unc.edu/tips-and-tools/changing-habits/

Cherry, K. (2024a, February 22). *13 Types of Common Cognitive Biases That Might Be Impairing Your Judgment.* Verywell Mind. https://www.verywellmind.com/cognitive-biases-distort-thinking-2794763

Cherry, K. (2024b, May 7). *How cognitive biases influence the way you think and act.* Verywell Mind. https://www.verywellmind.com/what-is-a-cognitive-bias-2794963

Cherry, K. (2025, February 11). *How to Be Open-Minded and Why It Matters.* Verywell Mind. https://www.verywellmind.com/be-more-open-minded-4690673

Chevallier, A., Dalsace, F., & Barsoux, J.-L. (2024, May 1). *The Art of Asking Smarter Questions.* Harvard Business Review. https://hbr.org/2024/05/the-art-of-asking-smarter-questions

Connors, H. (2023, May 15). *20 Healthy Mindset Habits To Improve Your Wellbeing.* The Intention Habit. https://theintentionhabit.com/healthy-mindset-habits/

Critical Conversations. (n.d.). Learning to Give. Retrieved May 20, 2025, from https://www.learningtogive.org/resources/critical-conversations

Critical thinking: Fostering Critical Thinking to Combat Groupthink. (2025, April 8). Faster Capi-

tal. https://fastercapital.com/content/Critical-thinking--Fostering
-Critical-Thinking-to-Combat-Groupthink.html

Decision-making process. (n.d.). University of Massachusetts Dartmouth.
Retrieved May 20, 2025, from https://www.umassd.edu/fycm/deci
sion-making/process/

Dipak Ahirav. (2025, January 8). *How I Learned to Celebrate Progress
Over Perfection.* Medium. https://medium.com/write-a-catalyst/ho
w-i-learned-to-celebrate-progress-over-perfection-df57678c8421

Dr. Menije. (2019). *What is Emotional Reasoning.* In YouTube. https
://www.youtube.com/watch?v=nvMRQxQqJXo

Dunne, K. (n.d.). *SWOT Analysis.* Mindtools. Retrieved May 20, 2025,
from https://www.mindtools.com/amtbj63/swot-analysis

Durham, S. P. (2019, September 2). *Why your Gut Feeling is more Powerful than Logic.* Medium. https://seanpatrickdurham.medium.com
/why-your-gut-feeling-is-more-powerful-than-logic-b1574d89936

Dwyer, C. (2018, September 7). *12 Common Biases That Affect How We
Make Everyday Decisions.* Psychology Today.
https://www.psychologytoday.com/za/blog/thoughts-on-thinking/
201809/12-common-biases-that-affect-how-we-make-everyday-decis
ions

Evaluating Evidence. (n.d.). Lumen Learning. https://courses.lumenle
arning.com/olemiss-writ250/chapter/evaluating-evidence/

42 Douglas Adams quotes to live by. (n.d.). BBC Radio 4. Retrieved May
20, 2025, from https://www.bbc.co.uk/programmes/articles/2bcFf
Mt6rGLTPpbG0yLwPw0/42-douglas-adams-quotes-to-live-by

Garcia, C. (2022, September 22). *Use These 8 Elements of Thought for
Making Objective Decisions You Won't Regret.* Medium.
https://medium.com/change-your-mind/use-these-8-elements-of-th
ought-for-making-objective-decisions-you-wont-regret-d24e1974ce9

Goodman, M. (n.d.). *Systems Thinking: What, Why, When, Where, and How?* The Systems Thinker. Retrieved May 20, 2025, from https://thesystemsthinker.com/systems-thinking-what-w hy-when-where-and-how/

Gupta, S. (2025, February 15). *What's The Difference Between Hearing and Listening?* Verywell Mind. https://www.verywellm ind.com/hearing-vs-listening-what-s-the-difference-5196734

Hale, J. (2020, April 27). *Strategies to Improve Skeptical Thinking.* Skeptical Inquirer. https://skepticalinquirer.org/exclusive/strat egies-to-improve-skeptical-thinking/

Hasan, J. (2023, March 15). *Critical Thinking: How to Evaluate Information and Make Sound Judgments.* Linkedin. https://www.linkedin.com/pulse/critical-thinking-ho w-evaluate-information-make-sound-hasan/

He who asks a question is a fool for five minutes; he who does not ask a question remains a fool forever. (2015, September 1). P h i l o s i b l o g . https://philosiblog.com/2015/09/01/he-who-asks-a-question-is -a-fool-for-five-minutes-he-who-does-not-ask-a-question-remain s-a-fool-forever/

High Quality Assignment Help. (2023, July 3). *Improving Critical Thinking: Strategies for Analyzing and Evaluating Information.* M e d i u m . https://highqualityassignmenthelp.medium.com/improving-crit ical-thinking-strategies-for-analyzing-and-evaluating-informatio n-ecec399335c2

Hintikka, J. J. (2025, March 27). *Logic.* Encyclopedia Britannica. https://www.britannica.com/topic/logic

Ho, L. (2025, February 19). *How to Combat Information Overload in the Digital Age.* Lifehack. https://www.lifehack.org/922480/inf ormation-overload

Hogsette, D. S. (2011). *Developing Critical Thinking with Journal Writing.* New York Institute of Technology. https://site.nyit.ed u/ctl/blog/critical_thinking_journal_writing

How Does Technology Affect Critical Thinking? (n.d.). Critical Thinking Secrets. Retrieved May 20, 2025, from https://criticalthinkin gsecrets.com/how-does-technology-affect-critical-thinking/

How to Clear Mental Clutter. (n.d.). Living with Margins. Retrieved May 20, 2025, from https://www.livingwithmargins.com/blog/ how-to-clear-mental-clutter

Indeed Editorial Team. (2024, August 17). *What Is Problem Analysis?* (With Processes and Useful Types). Indeed. https://ca.indeed .com/career-advice/career-development/problem-analysis

Indeed Editorial Team. (2025a, March 4). *15 Types of Thinking (Plus How To Find Your Type).* Indeed. https://www.indeed.com/caree r-advice/career-development/type-of-thinking

Indeed Editorial Team. (2025b, March 4). *How To Improve Your Logical Reasoning Skills (Plus Types).* Indeed. https://www.indeed.com/career-advice/career-developme nt/improve-your-logical-reasoning

Indeed Editorial Team. (2025c, March 26). *How To Structure An Effective Argument in 5 Steps.* Indeed. https://www.indeed.com/ career-advice/career-development/how-to-structure-an-argument

Ipsen, A. (2023, September 6). *How to improve your team's critical thinking skills.* Plural Sight. https://www.pluralsight.com/resources/blog/business-an d-leadership/how-improve-critical-thinking-skills-organization

John Foster Dulles Quotes. (n.d.). Brainy Quote. Retrieved May 20, 2025, from https://www.brainyquote.com/quotes/john_foster_du lles_163652

Katz, L. (2025, April 18). *The Ultimate Guide to Open-Ended Questions vs. Closed-Ended Questions.* Clear Voice. https://www.clearvoice.co m/resources/open-ended-questions-vs-closed-questions/

Keiling, H. (2025, April 29). *Inductive vs. Deductive Reasoning.* Indeed. https://www.indeed.com/career-advice/career-development/i nductive-vs-deductive-reasoning

Khan Academy. (2020). *Evaluating a source's reasoning and evidence.* In YouTube. https://www.youtube.com/watch?v=v4HhzvSgUpU

Knachel, M. (2020). *What is Logic?* Rebus Community. https://press. rebus.community/intro-to-phil-logic/chapter/chapter-1/

Kotsides, D. (2022, August 18). I*dentifying the problem is 50% of the solution.* Kalexius. https://www.kalexius.com/identifying-problem-so lution/

Kramer, L. (2023, April 10). *15 Logical Fallacies to Know, With Definitions and Examples.* Grammarly. https://www.grammarly.com/blo g/rhetorical-devices/logical-fallacies/

Lanese, N., Weisberger, M., & Bradford, A. (2024, March 6). *What's the difference between deductive reasoning and inductive reasoning?* Live Science. https://www.livescience.com/21569-deduction-vs-ind uction.html

Laoyan, S. (2025, January 17). *7 Important Steps of the Decision Making Process.* Asana. https://asana.com/resources/decision-making-proce ss

Magee, J. F. (1964, July). *Decision Trees for Decision Making.* Harvard Business Review. https://hbr.org/1964/07/decision-trees-for-decisi on-making

Maria George. (2024). *Difference between Deductive and Inductive Reasoning.* In YouTube. https://www.youtube.com/watch?v=lE duWUPFNMw

Marie Forleo. (2016). *How To Make The Right Decision When Your Gut And Logic Don't Agree.* In YouTube. https://www.youtube .com/watch?v=5TosxVEMMzM

Martins, J. (2024, August 30). *How to build your critical thinking skills in 7 steps (with examples).* Asana. https://asana.com/resou rces/critical-thinking-skills

Meyer, C. (n.d.). *25 Powerful Critical Thinking Quotes. The Mind Collection.* Retrieved May 20, 2025, from https://themindcollec tion.com/critical-thinking-quotes/

Milberg, D. (2016, January 15). *Systems Thinking: A better way of problem-solving.* Linkedin. https://www.linkedin.com/pulse/sys tems-thinking-better-way-problem-solving-dan-milberg/

Mindtools Content Team. (n.d.). *How to Keep Calm in a Crisis.* Mindtools. https://www.mindtools.com/agalv48/how-to-ke ep-calm-in-a-crisis

Mosunic, C. (n.d.). *How to stay calm under pressure (and how to be calm in everyday life).* Calm. Retrieved May 20, 2025, from https://www.calm.com/blog/how-to-stay-calm-under-pressure

Nicodemus, R. (n.d.). *Decluttering Mental Clutter.* The Minimal-ists. Retrieved May 20, 2025, from https://www.theminimalists .com/mental/

Nox, F. (2023, April 26). *The Importance of Curiosity: Why Maintaining an Open Mind is Essential for Personal Growth and Development.* Medium. https://medium.com/@francesconox/the-importance-of-curiosity

-why-maintaining-an-open-mind-is-essential-for-personal-growth-an
d-2922f01bb9d8

Ogolo, D. A. (2023, October 16). *Technology and Information Overload: Navigating the Digital Age.* Medium. https://medium.com/@makemoneyogb/technology-and-infor
mation-overload-navigating-the-digital-age-c6ddfc69cd45

Peer Pressure: How Groupthink Impacts Rational Thought. (2025, April
8). Faster Capital. https://fastercapital.com/content/Peer-Pressure
--How-Groupthink-Impacts-Rational-Thought.html

Piellusch, M. J. (2017, January 1). *Critical Thinking: Skepticism, Science,
and Sanity.* Linkedin. https://www.linkedin.com/pulse/critical-thi
nking-skepticism-science-sanity-ma-ms-dba/

Pilat, D., & Krastev, S. (n.d.-a). *Syllogism.* The Decision Lab. Retrieved
May 20, 2025, from https://thedecisionlab.com/reference-guide/ph
ilosophy/syllogism

Pilat, D., & Krastev, S. (n.d.-b). *Why Do We Favor Our Existing Beliefs?*
The Decision Lab. Retrieved May 20, 2025, from https://thedecisi
onlab.com/biases/confirmation-bias

Powers, B. (2023, May 3). *How to Ask Better Questions.*
Linkedin. https://www.linkedin.com/pulse/how-ask-better-questi
ons-bobby-powers/

Problem Solving. (n.d.). American Society for Quality. Retrieved May 20,
2025, from https://asq.org/quality-resources/problem-solving

*Quote Origin: I Would Spend 55 Minutes Defining the Problem and
then Five Minutes Solving It.* (2014, May 22). Quote Investigator.
https://quoteinvestigator.com/2014/05/22/solve/

A quote by Gautama Buddha. (n.d.). Goodreads. Retrieved May 20,
2025, from https://www.goodreads.com/quotes/1815-do-not-belie
ve-in-anything-simply-because-you-have-heard

A quote by Josh Billings. (n.d.). Goodreads. Retrieved May 20, 2025, from https://www.goodreads.com/quotes/189106-the-trouble-wit h-most-folks-isn-t-their-ignorance-it-s-knowin

Rochani, K. (2023, November 9). *Defining Problems: The Most Important Business Skill Often Overlooked.* Medi- um. https://medium.com/@karan_rochani/defining-problems-the -most-important-business-skill-often-overlooked-dfcdeb9e7d29

Schimelpfening, N. (2023, March 13). *Stress Can Affect Your Ability to Think Clearly, Study Finds.* Health- line. https://www.healthline.com/health-news/why-it-may-be-hard er-to-make-good-decisions-when-your-stressed

Scott, E. (2023, November 28). *6 Effective Ways to Clear Your Mind.* Verywell Mind. https://www.verywellmind.com/how-can-i-clear-m y-mind-3144602

Self-Awareness: Assumptions, Beliefs & Conditioning for Personal Growth. (2023, September 25). The Intentional Optimist. https://www.theintentionaloptimist.com/blog/episode-142-self-awa reness-uncovering-assumptions-beliefs-conditioning-for-personal-gr owth

Seltzer, L. F. (2017, June 21). *What's "Emotional Reasoning"—And Why Is It Such a Problem?* Psychology Today. https://www.psychologytoday.com/us/blog/evolution-of-the-self/2 01706/whats-emotional-reasoning-and-why-is-it-such-a-problem

7 Types of Thinking: How to Find Your Thinking Type. (2022, Novem- ber 23). Masterclass. https://www.masterclass.com/articles/types-of -thinking

SquareLink. (2018). *The lost art of making a sound argument (and how we can do better).* Steemit. https://steemit.com/philosophy/@phaazer1/the-lost-art-of-making

-a-sound-argument-and-how-we-can-do-better-part-1-in-a-square-link-blog-series-on-practical-critical

Streefkerk, R. (2019, April 18). *Inductive vs. Deductive Research Approach.* Scribbr. https://www.scribbr.com/methodology/inductive-deductive-reasoning/

Teach Thought Staff. (n.d.). *40 of the Best Quotes about Critical Thinking.* Teach Thought. Retrieved May 20, 2025, from https://www.teachthought.com/critical-thinking/quotes-critical-thinking/

The Foundation for Critical Thinking. (n.d.). *Critical Thinking in Everyday Life: 9 Strategies.* Critical Thinking. Retrieved May 20, 2025, from https://www.criticalthinking.org/pages/critical-thinking-in-everyday-life-9-strategies/512

The Macat Team. (2019, December 3). *10 examples of critical thinking that changed the world.* Macat International. https://www.macat.com/post/10-examples-of-critical-thinking-that-changed-the-world

30 Best Motivational Quotes by Great Leaders. (2023, December 27). Pragati Leadership. https://pragatileadership.com/30-best-motivational-quotes-by-great-leaders/

Thomas A. Edison Quotes. (n.d.). Brainy Quote. Retrieved May 20, 2025, from https://www.brainyquote.com/quotes/thomas_a_edison_132683

Traeger, S. (n.d.). *7 Powerful Root Cause Analysis Techniques and Tools.* Reliability. Retrieved May 20, 2025, from https://reliability.com/resources/articles/7-root-cause-analysis-technique/

Tsipursky, G. (2023, April 15). *12 Strategies To Defeat Cognitive Biases And Boost Your Bottom Line.* Forbes. https://www.forbes.com/sites/glebtsipursky/2023/04/15/12-strategies-to-defeat-cognitive-biases-and-boost-your-bottom-line/

Vettorazzi, C. (2022, January 5). *How I Declutter My Mind — Get More Clarity And Stop Feeling Overwhelmed.* Medium. https://medium.com/change-becomes-you/how-i-declutter-my-min d-get-more-clarity-and-stop-feeling-overwhelmed-4d912232ae38

Voltaire Quotes. (n.d.). Brainy Quote. Retrieved May 20, 2025, from https://www.brainyquote.com/quotes/voltaire_104483

Warley, S. (n.d.). *What Is Self-Awareness?* Life Skills That Matter. Retrieved May 20, 2025, from https://www.lifeskillsthatmatter.com/b log/self-awareness

What is a Decision Matrix? (n.d.). American Society for Quality. http s://asq.org/quality-resources/decision-matrix

Williams, R. (2024, January 3). *Should You Trust Logic and Data or Gut Feelings to Make Decisions?* Linkedin. https://www.linkedin.com/pulse/should-you-trust-logic -data-gut-feelings-make-ray-williams-kkbtc/

Wrike Team. (2021, January 25). *5 Tips to Make Collaborative Problem Solving Work for Your Team.* Wrike. https://www.wrike.com/blog/ 5-tips-make-collaborative-problem-solving-work-team/

Young, R. (2023, July 28). *The Power Of Critical Thinking: Enhancing Decision-Making And Problem-Solving.* Forbes. https://www.forbes.com/councils/forbescoachescouncil/2 023/07/28/enhancing-decision-making-and-problem-solving/

www.ingramcontent.com/pod-product-compliance
Lightning Source LLC
Chambersburg PA
CBHW070336130626
46556CB00007B/2883